HORSE SENSE AND THE HUMAN HEART

HORSE SENSE
and the
HUMAN HEART

What Horses Can Teach Us About Trust, Bonding, Creativity and Spirituality

Adele von Rüst McCormick, Ph.D., and
Marlena Deborah McCormick, Ph.D.

Health Communications, Inc.
Deerfield Beach, Florida

www.hci-online.com

Profits from this book are going to The Institute for Conscious/ Awareness, a nonprofit institute for psychospiritual exploration through nature and horses.

We are also donating a portion of the profits from this book to Trophaeum Mundi International,™ founded in 1992 by Jean-Philippe Giacomini. TMI is a nonprofit foundation devoted to developing an alternative to classical *dressage* competition and promoting the equestrian culture that flourished for centuries on the Iberian peninsula.

We would like to thank the following for permission to reprint their magnificent photographs: Lila Foucher, chapters 2, 4, 6, 7, 10; and Steven Giovannini, chapters 1, 5, 8, 9.

Library of Congress Cataloging-in-Publication Data

McCormick, Adele von Rüst, date
    Horse sense and the human heart : what horses can teach us about trust, bonding, creativity, and spirituality / Adele von Rüst McCormick and Marlena Deborah McCormick.
      p. cm.
    Includes bibliographical references and index.
    ISBN 1-55874-523-8 (pbk.)
    1. Horsemanship—Therapeutic use. 2. Psychotherapy. 3. Horses—Psychological aspects. 4. Human-animal relationships.
    I. McCormick, Marlena Deborah. II. Title.
    RC489.H67M38 1997
    616.89'165—dc21   97-35476
                                            CIP

Publisher: Health Communications, Inc.
           3201 S.W. 15th Street
           Deerfield Beach, Florida 33442-8190

Cover design by Lawna Patterson Oldfield
Cover photo ©1997 PhotoDisc, Inc.

*There should be no mediocrity in love,
and without love you cannot
create an Art.*

NUNO OLIVEIRA,
OLD MASTER TRAINER TO YOUNG TRAINERS

We dedicate this book to the two
champions in our lives . . .
Thomas E. McCormick, M.D.,
our inspiration,
and
F.P.C. Trianero,
our Peruvian mystic

CONTENTS

ACKNOWLEDGMENTS

We wish to express our great appreciation to all the wonderful people who have helped and supported us in the birth of our first book. Our heartfelt thanks go to Stephanie Marohn, friend and editor. Our thanks go also to our literary agent, Barbara Neighbors Deal: You are the best, Barbara. We also wish to thank our editor, Paulann Thurmon, for her patience and guidance, and our computer expert, Wilhelmina Grader-Stephens of The Paper Mill.

We extend our sincere thanks to Christine E. Belleris, our editor at Health Communications, and to Peter Vegso at Health Communications, for his vision and belief in the healing power of horses. To all the staff of Health Communications, we offer thanks for their direction, support and expertise. We also thank Heath Lynn Silberfeld for her skill and intuition in helping us polish the final draft of our book.

Our friends Arthur Hoffman, M.D., and Peter Tsantilis, Ph.D., were always behind us in the "treatment years." We are indebted to those who supported the philosophy of the book, including Mirian Frenk and José Poveda de Augustine,

Ph.D., M.D. To Jean-Philippe Giacomini, Dominique Barbier, Jean-Claude Racinet and José Risso Montes, thank you for supporting our dream. Our sincere thanks go also to Janetta Michael, executive director of the Peruvian Paso Horse Registry of North America.

Our dear friend Elaine Harrison, Esq., has supported us throughout the years. Thank you, too.

Our gratitude also goes to Larry Dossey, M.D., who not only endorsed us but believed in our horses as "four-legged partners." Our appreciation goes to Rupert Sheldrake, Ph.D., for his morphic resonance theory, and to Father William Rontani of Saint Luke's Episcopal Church in Calistoga, horse lover and spiritual guide.

We thank our wonderful veterinarian and friend, Dick Perce, D.V.M.

Last but not least, Adele wishes to remember, with gratitude, the late Dr. Jacob Levy Moreno, a man before his time who opened doors to the mystery of life.

And of course we are thankful to all our patients who taught us so much.

FOREWORD

s Edgar Mitchell explored the cosmos, Drs. Adele and Marlena Deborah McCormick explore the heart of nature and its creatures.

Throughout history, horses have helped humans navigate on their external travels. This book is about how horses can take us on another, deeper journey, to the realms of healing, awareness and soul growth.

Humans think of themselves as the most evolved species, yet the McCormicks have learned from their horses that these amazing animals can serve as teachers and guides, and transport us to a new journey of consciousness.

In this era of high-tech medical intervention for physical ailments and drug intervention for mental illness, there is a growing groundswell of interest in alternative approaches to healing and wholeness. One of the newest approaches is the use of animals in the therapeutic process. Researchers are exploring the healing effects generated by dogs in convalescent homes, tropical fish as stressbusters for the anxious and depressed, and the value of relationship with an animal for people recovering from heart attacks. The McCormicks' work takes human-animal interaction a leap further. They have discovered that in addition to facilitating healing, the horses teach us to look deeper into nature and our interconnectedness with all life, and as a result, deeper into our own hearts. In the company of horses, we can learn to develop that selfless love the Greeks called *agape*, which leads to a passion for life—a passion that has dimmed as we've lost our communion with nature and the natural.

Animals as diverse as llamas, rabbits and pot-bellied pigs have helped human beings recover from mental and physical illnesses. Elephants, gorillas, dolphins and pigeons, among many other creatures, have aided humans in distress. Dr. Rupert Sheldrake, whose recent work on interspecies communication has received worldwide attention, has written of the McCormicks' work: "Obviously there is a great deal of potential for horses, and other animals, to help people. The use of dogs and other smaller animals in hospitals has already shown this, but I am sure the experience of horses is even more powerful." The McCormicks have found this to be true; the sheer physical presence of a large animal like a horse evokes a different level and quality of experience in humans.

A look at some of these human-animal interactions, at animals as a source of healing in the therapeutic process, and at what appears to be animal concern for human welfare, provides a backdrop for the remarkable work of psychologists Adele and Marlena Deborah McCormick and their partners, the Peruvian Paso horses.

Over 2,000 therapy programs throughout the United States are using dogs with enviable bedside manners. Their owners bring them once a week to interact with patients like Marquette Buie, a young man who is recovering from gunshot wounds that left him quadriplegic in 1994. "When I was hurting and thought I couldn't go on," he says, "I'd come to see these dogs." Giving them verbal commands helped him regain the use of his voice, and tossing a rubber ball in a game of fetch helped him learn to use his right arm, hand and fingers.

The extent to which animals respond to humans in need is simply stunning. Peruvian Paso horses are amazing in their intuitive response to a disturbed youngster's need for trust. Others from all walks of life find the horses an inspiration to self-discovery and the exploration of expanded consciousness. Horses share this seemingly intuitive gift with many other animals.

Animal Helpers: Wild and Domestic

Binti Jua, an eight-year-old Western lowland gorilla with a baby on her back, grabbed headlines around the world when she rescued a three-year-old boy who fell 20 feet into the gorilla enclosure at the Brookfield Zoo in suburban Chicago, landing on his head. Heading off another gorilla, Binti picked up the child, cradled him in her arms, and placed him near a door where zookeepers could retrieve him. They sprayed water on the other gorillas to keep them away. The boy was admitted in critical condition to the Loyola University medical center, but was released within a week. [1]

Was Binti simply responding to blind biological instincts when she rescued the helpless child? Are we romanticizing animals to believe they really care about human welfare?

Commander David Blunt, who was Cultivation Protector for Tanganyika, now known as Tanzania, described how a local woman placed her baby in the shade of a tree while she worked.

Suddenly there was a crash in the brush as a herd of elephants passed by. When they reached the baby, they stopped. Two or three of the elephants began to pull branches from the tree and gently covered the baby with the foliage, being careful not to wake it. Then they moved off. The purpose of their action, Blunt believed, was to protect the infant from flies as it slept. [2]

When animals come to the aid of humans in distress, they often appear to invoke ways of knowing that currently defy explanation; this is especially clear in the McCormicks' work. Consider the events surrounding the disappearance in 1983 of Oscar Simonet, a three-year-old boy, from a picnic with his family along the rugged coast of Minorca. The frantic family presumed he had fallen off a rugged cliff. For 30 hours, search parties combed the area, and frogmen probed nearby inlets, to no avail. The search effort was organized by José Tadeo, the mayor of Villacarlos, the closest town. When the mayor returned to his house following the futile efforts, his Irish setter, Harpo, behaved strangely. Normally calm and obedient, he would not let Tadeo relax, but kept running to the front door and whining, as if he wanted to go outside. The mayor responded and followed as the dog led him toward the spot where the little boy had disappeared. Harpo stopped at a crevice hidden by underbrush, which the searchers had passed many times. Tadeo crashed through the tangled vegetation to find Oscar semiconscious. He had crawled into the undergrowth, fallen into the three-foot crevice, and hit his head on a rock. How did Harpo know the boy was missing? He was two miles away when the boy disappeared. How did he know the exact spot? Was this a "funny coincidence"? [3]

If so, there are a lot of them. And it isn't just domesticated animals that seem to recognize and respond to human distress.

In 1980, 82-year-old Miss Rachel Flynn took her customary walk on Cape Cod and fell off a 30-foot cliff onto a lonely beach. Too badly hurt to move, she thought she would die. Lying trapped between boulders, she saw a seagull hovering over her. She remembered that she and her sister had regularly fed a gull, which they named Nancy, at their home. Could this be the same bird? Acting on a long shot, Miss Flynn cried, "For God's sake, Nancy, get help."

The gull flew off toward her home, a mile away, where June, her sister, was working in the kitchen. June described later that she was irritated by a seagull that began tapping on the windowpane with its beak and flapping its wings, "making more noise than a wild turkey." She could not shoo it away. After 15 minutes of the gull's frantic behavior, it occurred to June that the wild bird—it was not a pet—might be trying to tell her something. Going outside, she followed the bird as it flew ahead. It stopped occasionally, as if to make sure she was following. The seagull alighted on the cliff over which Miss Flynn had fallen. June summoned an ambulance, which rescued her bruised and helpless sister. [4]

Monkeys, too, have been known to help humans in need. Sergeant Cyril Jones, a Welshman now in his 80s, parachuted into Sumatra in 1942, in an attempt to stall the Japanese advance across Southeast Asia. He became snagged in a tree, where he hung for 12 days, unable to cut himself down. He would have died except for a monkey who befriended him and brought him food. "We became very close friends and the monkey started bringing me bananas," Jones recalled. "Sometimes he would bring me bamboo shoots, which he showed me how to eat." Jones finally managed to free himself, but the monkey followed him and continued to bring him fruit. When he was captured by the Japanese, the monkey followed him to the prison camp and turned on the Japanese captors when they tried to bully Jones. Jones's experience resulted in an affection for monkeys but an aversion to bananas. "I was sick to death of them," he relates. "It was a long time before I could eat them again." [5]

Donald Mottram, a Welsh farmer, owes his life to Daisy, one of his favorite cows. When he ventured into a field to attend a calf, he noticed a Charolais bull 300 yards away, but assumed it was shepherding the calf and thought nothing of it. Suddenly he was hurled 30 feet in the air. When he recovered in a daze, the bull was trampling him and kicked him unconscious. Ninety minutes later, when he came to, his herd—apparently marshalled by 14-year-old Daisy, one of his favorite cows—had surrounded him, while the bull could be heard stamping and bellowing outside the protective circle. With the herd shielding him, Mottram crawled 200 yards to the gate. He was hospitalized for six days with broken ribs and injuries to his lungs and shoulders. "They say cows are dumb creatures," he said later, "but I'm certain my animals knew of the danger I was in and decided to protect me. Some of my favorite cows were in the group—as well as Daisy there was Megan, Amy, Bethan, Mary and Kitty. They undoubtedly saved me from being trampled to death." [6]

Peruvian Paso Horses as Therapists and Teachers

In this book, you hold in your hands an account of one of the most innovative, exciting and effective methods ever devised to help severely emotionally disturbed teenagers. The

McCormicks, of Calistoga, California, employ Peruvian Paso horses as an integral aspect of psychotherapy when traditional approaches fail. Adele and Marlena Deborah, mother and daughter, are psychotherapists. Their "office" is a stable and riding ring at Three Eagles Ranch.

These amazingly intuitive horses bring healing to troubled young people. Even kids with the greatest challenges and most severe damage—sociopaths, psychopaths, children from horrendously abusive situations, hardened gang members— find that bonding with horses touches that which is most deeply human within themselves, and helps them build bridges of trust—first with the horses and then with the McCormicks. With lots of hard work and compassionate interaction, these young people find a way out of their disease to become whole, productive members of society.

However, it isn't just disturbed youngsters who learn from the horses. Peruvian Pasos also inspire healthy adults and young people to explore new levels of trust, bonding, creativity and spirituality. The McCormicks and the horses now spe-cialize in working with clients in the areas of self-discovery, opening intuition and expanding creativity. This program, called the Equine Experience, nurtures and inspires partici-pants to new levels of success in their work and relationships, and deeper growth in their inner lives.

In these pages you will explore the rich and ancient history of the partnership between humans and horses. You'll take a psychologist's-eye-view of how humans develop feelings and emotions, and how, through internal or external damage, what should be normal, healthy emotional growth can mutate to dysfunction.

The fascinating subjects of instinct and intuition are

plumbed, as is the role animals play in teaching us about intimacy, bonding, and belonging. For generations we've spoken
of the quality of wisdom described as "horse sense." The
McCormicks give us a clear understanding of this much
admired trait, and how, if we attend to the ways horses are
true to their own natures, we can embody a uniquely human
"horse sense" of our own.

Horses are especially effective in helping people understand and overcome fear and aggression, bringing harmony
and alignment between the unconscious and conscious mind,
and developing conscience and an awareness of the effects of
one's behavior on others. Through their uncanny ability to
"mirror," horses spark a deeper understanding of our behavior,
and inspire us to a more spiritual, mystical and philosophical
orientation to life.

The final section of this book asks perceptive questions about
the nature of spirituality and creativity. The horses can teach us
what nurtures the creative impulse and point us to unity with all
life and with God. All healing springs from the one Source, and
this book offers with great clarity a path open to humans to
reconnect with our intuitive core and with our natural heritage.

This account is rich with examples and case histories that
bring the principles of healing and wholeness to life. Whether
or not you ever meet a horse face-to-face, you can employ the
principles that the McCormicks have learned while working
with their four-legged partners.

What Is This Human-Animal Bond?

When we develop a special relationship with a nonhuman
creature, we experience something mysterious, something not

easily understood—the "human-animal bond," researchers call it. What is this bond? What is being bonded? Why does the bondedness feel good, and why is it good for health?

Animals provide us the opportunity to unite unconditionally with another living being. They teach us to love. Love, in a general sense, involves a relaxing of personal boundaries and a willingness to "become one" with someone else. Love, to flourish, requires surrendering our rigid sense of individuality that creates distance and separateness.

Perhaps we do not "develop" a bond with animals or with each other; our bondedness is fundamental, natural, factory-installed, the way things are. Of course it doesn't feel that way most of the time, because through the processes of enculturation, individuation and socialization we learn to devalue and ignore our bondedness with others. Animals bring us back to the realization of our unity with other living things. They help us remember who we are.

Samuel Butler (1835-1902) said, "The great pleasure of a dog is that you may make a fool of yourself with him and not only will he not scold you, but he will make a fool of himself too." [7] Animals give us permission to remove our masks and behave naturally. Is this how they open doors to love? The McCormicks have discovered this to be true with their horse partners.

"Consciousness is nonlocal," states physicist Amit Goswami of the Department of Physics and Institute of Theoretical Science at the University of Oregon in Eugene. [8] That is, it is not restricted to specific points in space, such as individual brains or bodies, or to specific points in time, such as the present moment. Consciousness, rather, in this view is infinite in space and time, bridging between distant individuals and other conscious creatures as well. Does nonlocal mind make possible the human-animal bond? Is this why animals and humans can find each other across great distances, as if they are in contact no matter how far apart? Rupert Sheldrake, a pioneer explorer of the human-animal bond, describes this ability as a function of what he calls morphic resonance and morphogenetic fields. "The presence of morphogenetic fields provides a way for all thoughts to become linked across space and time. This is a picture of nonlocal and transpersonal mind, and a way for individual minds to communicate. . . . Experiments with animals seem to indicate that telepathy or morphic resonance . . . occurs not just between humans, but between humans and animals as well." [9]

We can explain some of the elements of the human-animal bond through conventional psychological concepts, such as the acceptance, nonjudgment and companionship offered by other creatures. But the bond may be more fundamental than we have imagined, and may involve the nature of consciousness itself. [10]

Philosopher George Jaidar describes this bond as a process —*Umbilicum process*. "This is not an entity, but a dynamic, metabiological, transexperiential, communicative network process by means of which members of a species transmit and receive 'learnings' to and from one another through and from . . . the Source. *I would also include interspecies and extraspecies communion and communication* [italics added]. The Umbilicum process can be seen as nonlocal organizing fields that both transmit and receive information to and from our world of existence. . . ." [11]

We shall never be able to understand our most dramatic connections with animals—those that transcend space and time, and those that bring healing to humans—until we entertain a nonlocal view of the mind. This particular view of consciousness is being taken seriously in modern science, psychology and philosophy.

In today's high-tech health care environment, it is ironic that a puppy's sloppy kiss can create measurable health benefits, and that bonding with a horse can create a model, a template that enables a troubled teen to bond with another person or inspires a healthy adult to explore new dimensions of spirituality. Yet the evidence favoring the healing value of animals is so compelling that if animal therapy were a pill, we would not be able to manufacture it fast enough. It would be available in every hospital, mental health clinic, spiritual growth center and nursing home in the land. When a person entered such a facility, the opportunity to have contact with a caring animal would be routine. In view of the data that is available, we can well ask, What's the holdup?

Larry Dossey, M.D., and Barbara Neighbors Deal, Ph.D.

Portions of this foreword are adapted from *The Healing Power of Pets: A Look at Animal-Assisted Therapy* by Larry Dossey, M.D., an editorial in the July, 1997 (volume 3, number 4) issue of *Alternative Therapies*.

INTRODUCTION

Under these conditions nature can be felt
as something that gives a sense of the whole that
goes far beyond the individual or the collective.

—David Bohm and Mark Edwards,
Changing Consciousness

Working with serious mental illness, criminal behavior and substance addiction over the years has forced us to travel into interpersonal realms where few have gone. Over and over, we have had to face our own feelings of vulnerability, helplessness, fear and despair, only to find that, in the end, there is hope. Our experiences, although sometimes terrifying, compelled us to look deep inside ourselves, where we found an unexpected peace. It is through this upheaval and self-scrutiny that we have come to know joy.

As therapists, it was a surprise to find out that so much of what we learned academically had so little to do with the reality of working with severely disturbed people. Not once

during our academic careers were we ever realistically prepared for the roller-coaster nature of the professional path we
were setting out on. We were not told of the horror, the helplessness or the elation we would feel in treating maladies of
the human heart. So, when we launched our practice, it was
trial by fire. When we were finally faced with patients in the
depths of despair or the throes of violence—a humbling experience—we learned we had to drop the professional persona
and rely on our own intuition. There is no therapeutic technique that can save you in these situations. You come to rely
on your own feelings and pure instinct. These became our
most valuable tools. This awareness set us on a metaphysical
path and heightened our spirituality.

Tearing down walls of fear and defensiveness is a great challenge. When we were honest with ourselves about what really
helped people, we realized it was not just psychotherapy.
There was no getting around the fact that our best, most successful interventions were usually done by the seat of our
pants. They were never well thought-out or in keeping with
good theoretical form, but resulted from pure instinct and
intuition, orchestrated more perhaps by the grace of God
than by us. And God knows, in many instances we needed all
the grace we could get. After many successes, we realized that
there were other forces at work—forces that are rarely considered. This is where our real story began. It is about those
ever-present forces we all forget to tap into. We now know
that the healing process occurs when it is natural and a part
of life, rather than contrived. For this to happen, it must contain elements of enchantment and mystery.

In our practice we had worked with many people whom
others in our profession considered hopeless. We had grown

used to and welcomed challenges. They helped us stretch our minds and our imaginations and devise new approaches to our work. We searched for unique ways to wake up ourselves and others, to heal and to create healthy excitement in our lives. In our search, we were led to horses—animals that had always been part of our personal lives. This shift was slow and subtle. The methods that evolved seemed to emerge on their own, transporting us into new territory, professionally and personally.

We had always kept horses because we adored them and enjoyed their companionship. Although they had provided us with much welcome pleasure over the years, we never imagined what living intimately with the herd could do for the human psyche. Horses kept appearing in our dreams and imaginations. These images, combined with our professional experiences, were leading us deeper into the realms of nature.

We made a leap in faith and followed our dreams to the country, leaving our conventional practice and the urban treadmill behind us. A few of our colleagues were extremely supportive and wished us well. Most thought we were just plain crazy. Crazy or not, we and our clients have benefited immensely from what followed.

Our efforts began in a small way and gained momentum. We attuned ourselves to nature's pulse by living among horses and, to the extent possible, becoming part of the herd. We made this experience available to our clients with an aim to facilitate what we term "disciplined play."

With time, we recognized that a healing process was taking place, through the horses' relationships with us and our clients. What we discovered through this unconventional medium was a link to life in its rawest form. Working with horses, we initiated our clients into the hidden world of animal energy and instinct, providing them with a safe and natural means of learning about their own dualistic natures. The therapist/ horse/client interaction restored the mind, body and spirit to a state of wholeness. Through training in the form of disciplined play with horses, clients learned to tap into their ancient "animal" mind and energies and apply them toward more creative and responsible living. In fact, clients assumed responsibility for their own healing.

Observing and interacting with nonhuman animals can be a transforming experience and a powerful tool for igniting personal growth. The animal world is remarkable in its undistorted government by natural law. It is a world of cycles and seasons and ordered, adaptive movement. Even the quiet vibrates. Life and death go hand in hand, and this primordial embrace confers a quality of passion and immediacy to a realm from which the human animal is strangely distanced through intellect and delusion. Regardless of life's vicissitudes, animals always manage to struggle, love, establish relationships, play, raise their young and mourn their dead.

The horse's peculiar constellation of characteristics introduces health into a relationship. It is a well-balanced animal. Among domesticated animals selected for traits humans favor, horses have retained a strong component of their original wild nature. Because they're not so eager to please as domesticated dogs, they're less labile and more strong-willed. They are also fiercely independent. Their imposing size, tremendous strength and keen intuition require that one approach them with respect, vigilance and a great deal of sensitivity. One must also become highly attuned to them physically, and it's important to stay conscious and very much in the moment, allowing inner feelings to arise and verbalizing them. Once a good relationship is established with a horse, the interactions are exhilarating and liberating.

In our own interactions with horses we discovered a force—an unseen but ever-present energy that bathes the spirit and requires that we be completely present and true to our own nature. A horse's ability to connect with people is uncanny. Its size and presence somehow force us to become physically, mentally and spiritually more aware and more human. This elevated state of consciousness leads to renewed sensitivity and excitement, quite literally bringing us to our senses.

We were struck with the healing properties inherent in our interactions with these animals. The nature of the psychological and spiritual impact the horses had on us and on others was in keeping with many of our ideas about bringing people to better emotional, physical and spiritual health. We began to see horses as a natural and practical vehicle for developing self-awareness, a tool for calling attention to feelings that may be underdeveloped or out of balance. We feel that in this work we tap into an unconscious realm—one that we often forget in maneuvering our way through a largely artificial environment.

When we began working with horses 15 years ago, we had no idea of their potential as holistic healers that could help people experience the instinctual sides of themselves, physically as well as psychologically. Our work taught us that the horses were skillful guides, divine messengers in a sense, who can show us who we are and point us in the direction we need to go. They act as larger-than-life-size mirrors, reflecting back to us the totality of who we are, complete with light and shadow.

Throughout history and across civilizations, horses have been deemed one of the most noble creatures in the animal kingdom. They embody living, breathing desire and hold the key to the door of eternal passion. In the ancient Druid culture, horses were thought to take people on inner journeys and to help them negotiate the path of life and death. In this book, we will travel in all senses of the word. This adventure will unveil the ancient and arcane wisdom horses have to give us.

Through working with adult felons and paroled juvenile gang members in the 1960s, we developed a model of how healthy feeling evolves. We viewed feelings as guides on the secret journeys of our individual souls. If we learn to understand them, regardless of whether they cause us pain or pleasure, we can gain self-knowledge, or "gnosis." This, in turn, unlocks the door to spiritual development. Feeling, or sentiment, is the province of the heart, not the intellect, and its development ultimately leads to a sense of compassion and a heightened, accessible form of intuition. This realm of experience fosters a sense of humility and responsibility toward other beings.

Many of the criminal offenders with whom we worked had a severely limited repertoire of expressed feelings. Often, what they termed a feeling would be more accurately characterized as an emotion. Emotion, as the word is used in this book, is a display or performance that is devoid of sentimental content and is characteristic of psychopathic personalities. It is used to manipulate others and is a con.

People who use emotion, as distinct from expressing feeling, often lack personal insight, empathy and intuition, and consequently are strangers to their own impulses and behaviors. Many offenders who readily admit to having committed a crime have little or no awareness of why they committed it. They typically state, "Something just clicked." They have a sense of being driven by uncontrollable urges. It is this unaware acting out that makes them such a danger to themselves and others. Criminal offenders do have a heightened energy, but it is a rather dark side of passion in that it's often unbridled, unneutralized and running amok.

Through our years of clinical practice with patients diagnosed as psychotic, we've found that these individuals display emotion/feeling extremes opposite those seen in criminal offenders. That is, they tend to be inundated by feelings and a heightened sensitivity, or hypervigilance. Unable to realistically confront their pain, they resort to fantasy and create delusions and hallucinations to cope with the overwhelming flood of feeling. Psychotics have no reality-based means of organizing and understanding the maelstrom that is their internal process. Lacking a psychological mechanism to screen out excessive stimulation, they are prone to psychological collapse, or implosion. Early in their psychosis, they are adroit at straddling inner and outer reality. But eventually the real world becomes unbearable and they learn to escape essentially through mind travel.

Both psychopaths and psychotics share a basic characteristic—a lack of the awareness of their own internal process and behavior that is key to developing a well-integrated self. Understanding these two general groupings is important because they represent opposite ends of a continuum of feeling, between which most of the rest of the population falls. This model lets us assess our own feeling repertoire and affords useful insights in self-discovery. If we cultivate and integrate the various levels of feeling available to us, we can open ourselves to a richness of experience we've not felt before. Conversely, if we ignore these levels, leaving them untapped, they shroud the personality in darkness and confusion.

We used our observations of these feeling levels to help not only people seeking help, but their therapists as well, become more aware and balanced. We discovered that, whether they were established professionals or interns in training, therapists who used these feeling levels effectively had far more success in their work. When they began to shift their own feelings unconsciously, they began to empathize more fully with the feeling tone/level of their clients.

This patient population was once our primary concern and the focus of our practice. We have always searched for unique ways to reach others, help them heal and create their own excitement in life. Today our approach to therapeutic practice is based on this model, and we've had the opportunity to use it with many clients who didn't respond to conventional types of therapy. We bring this model to you in the hope that you, too, will find the passion, excitement and self-awareness we have found.

Over the years, we have designed and implemented a number of programs for diverse age groups, including gang youths, substance abusers, people struggling with depression and those exploring their spirituality. Today we run individualized programs or retreats for anyone seeking enrichment and a more meaningful life. We have found these particularly effective for people who are under excessive stress. The Equine Experience is the essence of all these programs.

This book describes a way we have found to again make living an art form. In our personal and professional lives, re-establishing a true and deep connection with nature— through horses—has been the most effective and effortless path toward reclaiming lost spirit and passion. Horses can be instrumental in helping transmute raw, instinctual urges into creative enterprise, and in putting the heart and passion back into life as we let go of old habits. We invite our readers to join us on our path of discovery—to become the involved self.

The names of the program participants used throughout this book have been changed to protect their privacy.

1

The Classic Horse

There is no secret so close
as that between a rider
and his horse.

—Surtees, circa 800 A.D.

Since childhood we have all had encounters with the Classic Horse. It is the horse of our dreams, fanciful and airborne, with a long flowing mane and tail. Its nostrils flare, displaying an inner spirit as magnificent as the mighty wind. It is the waves of the ocean and the fire of the setting sun. It saves us from the world. This mythic horse has marched forever through time with humans. This enduring image is a catalyst, opening us up to new horizons and teaching us about our inner feelings, the doorway to intuition. The Classic Horse rings in our psyche like a church bell; its overtones reverberate and linger, long after the bell has rung.

No one knows how our friendship with the horse began, but we do know a deep affection and camaraderie exist. Throughout time horses have been powerful archetypes, giving humans direction as they venture into the labyrinths of the soul. Over the centuries horses, being natural travelers, have faithfully accompanied people on journeys, external and internal. The horse has willingly carried us to faraway places, to enchanted castles, to and from battle, and even to the grave. It has accompanied us to new frontiers and joined us on heroic adventures.

The ancient Celts, Greeks, Indo-Europeans, Iberians, Berbers, Persians and Asians knew horses embodied a healing metaphor and reflected that belief in the rich mythology surrounding horses. The ancients called them messengers between ourselves and the divine, companions to the gods.

Even today urbanization has not killed human affinity for this mythic horse. Its mystery, allure and healing attributes live on. We discovered that involvement with real horses, particularly ancient breeds like the Iberians, stimulate this age-old archetype. In modern times the lore surrounding Iberian horses continues unabated. In Portugal, the horse is revered as the "Son of the Wind" who came out of the sea from the lost continent of Atlantis and is imbued with the same magical qualities as its ancestor, the unicorn. Aware or not, humankind has been raised on these horse stories and they are an inseparable part of the human psyche. Remember Black Beauty, the Black Stallion, Roy Rogers and Trigger, the Red Pony, and the great El Cid? The Classic Horse awakens the human heart to the essence of a love the ancient Greeks called *agape*—a complete and all-encompassing love of the creator and the created, a love difficult to practice as it is so selfless. Yet we can grow closer to it if we listen to the voice of the Classic Horse.

One can ride this horse in spirit only. You can ride, watch, read, imagine or just think about this Classic Horse, and during times of stress summon it as a source of comfort and guidance. Close your eyes and see yourself in the saddle of this strong and noble animal. When you do, you become strong and majestic as well. Listen to its hooves hitting the ground, a living drum. Each hoofbeat resounds in a four-beat quatrain, the rhythm many great poets use to turn words into music. Listen to what the horse is saying to you. Ride up and down the valleys, in the meadows, beside streams, through vineyards and where the mustard grows. Notice the ever-changing scenery, the vastness and the beauty of nature.

As you read on, continue to imagine yourself with a horse. Its knowing eyes, the way it runs to you, its size as well as its gentility. You feel this friendship is a privilege. Whisper and receive acknowledgment. As the horse knickers and prances to you, you feel special. It is with you to warn of impending danger and defend you in times of need.

Most important, listen to the breathing and heartbeat of your gallant horse. What color is it, how does it hold its head? Turn this into your own power-guided imagery. Now open your eyes, take deep breaths, and read on.

This book is a way to enter the real and fanciful world of Classic Horses and understand their longstanding spiritual relationship with humankind. When the rider or participant resonates feelings with a horse, healing occurs. The healing relationship is a reciprocal one in body and spirit. Through the mind/body connection, horses help and invigorate many people from all walks of life, whether couples, individuals or people in business, whether under stress or advancing in spiritual development. What more wonderful way to actually enter a myth or a legend and become part of the herd than on the back of a noble horse? There we can begin to loosen our mechanical materialism and soften to the voices of nature, the psyche of the cosmos. When we give up control and let the horse be our guide, we can rediscover our souls.

In our equine program, we use Spanish-Peruvian horses as the breed of choice because they are ancient, loving, intelligent and expressive, and have a smooth, natural gait. The bounce-free ride, as opposed to the jarring motion of the trot, helps new riders feel more comfortable in the saddle. As one sits centered on this horse, whether real or imagined, one moves into a meditative state.

In every age, individuals looking to expand their experience have undertaken a pilgrimage. The trials and tribula-
tions encountered along the way shape their character. In our
world we seldom have an opportunity for such transformative
journeys. The Equine Experience is one such avenue. The
people you'll meet in this book have ventured down this road,
and the lessons learned are memorable. Many tell us that
horses, being heroic by nature, stir something new inside and
inspire a quest for the divine.

The horse acts as a mirror, reflecting us back to ourselves,
and thus is a powerful assistant in the pursuit of self-realization.
Many people who experience this firsthand come away feeling
something uncanny has happened. It is a concrete way to see
universal forces at work within our being. What we uncover is
our own inner essence in bold, living color.

One very capable professional woman was overly demanding with others. Supercilious around her family, she was driving them away. Paula's competency over the years had made
her impatient with their shortcomings. Hoping to bring the
family closer together, she decided to get a Peruvian horse for
recreation. Up until that time, she felt superior and flawless.
However, the sweet Peruvian gelding performed for everyone
in the family except her. In consultation with us, we watched
her ride. Off a horse she was composed and competent. On a
horse, it was a different story. The horse knew she was faking
it. The minute Paula mounted, her back stiffened. She
bounced up and down in the saddle like a pogo stick, and so
did the horse.

Riding always uncovers a mind/body connection. Paula's
intellect could cover her apprehension and lack of confidence,
but her body exposed her inner fear. Once she could see her

fear via the jerky movements of the horse, her denial vanished. She became more humble, human and easier to live with.

Sam, a middle-aged man, had been taking lessons with us for some time and loved the horses. During this time his wife became terminally ill, and he was very worried. Horses became the highlight of his week, giving him the emotional fuel to carry on his caretaking role. Sam never wanted to burden anyone with his problems but was on the verge of complete exhaustion. He carried his load silently and stoically, forgetting to attend to any of his own feelings and needs. When friends asked if they could help, he always said, "No, everything is all right, everything is under control."

While taking a lesson one day he was having trouble getting the mare to go straight. She would weave in and out and then speed up and slow down. She was not dangerous but was frantic and inconsistent. Saying very little, we waited. Sam stopped the horse and said, "I can hide my anxiety from everyone, but not from the horses. Whenever I am with the horses they know how I feel. She knows I am terrified about what is happening in my life, even if I can't admit it."

Horses for Horseless People

In watching horses we found that when they are content and relaxed, we also feel relaxed. When they get excited, we get excited. For a variety of reasons, we humans are captivated by them. Spellbound by their graceful movement and boundless spirit, strong waves of energy are exchanged by way of intense identification. Most people can be moved by simply observing horses. This awareness led us to make films of horses for people who are shut in and can't leave their beds, houses or institutions. Many of these people say the films carry them into a dimension of peace and joy, even when troubled, and that they savor the experience and come away feeling their life is more enriched. People who have shut the world out can develop trust, motivation and hope through this medium. It reconnects them to nature and brings in the world. After watching the films, many want to make a trip to see the horses "in person."

Richard and Joseph were both invalids who had been shut-ins for years. They both had debilitating illnesses, and their world had become very confined. Richard suffered from massive heart failure, and Joseph, severe arthritis. Joseph needed an operation but could not leave Richard alone without care. Years ago, paralyzed by a fear of death, Richard gave up the idea of ever leaving his bed again. Both tried to stay mentally active in their one-room apartment. Keeping each other company was a big part of their day, along with watching movies, reading and studying metaphysics.

Sadly, most of their friends stopped coming over. Through our Circle of Light group, we started visiting with stories, pictures and videos of the horses. Over a period of time they began to know each horse by name and personality. They eagerly awaited news from the ranch, like the birth of a foal. Becoming very involved, they knew the horses as well as anyone. Yet as time went on they longed to "meet the horses" someday.

As this desire grew, Richard and Joseph started thinking differently about themselves and their lives. Richard is now in rehabilitation, learning to walk, so Joseph can have his operation. Their overriding goal is to visit the ranch and be with the horses. The vicarious experience sparked a desire within them to become active again. We learned that horses can have a strong affect on people even through the media. In this case the horses were enough to inspire Richard and Joseph to begin taking charge and to heal themselves.

Since horses communicate with their skin, we find that simply touching them also heals. The blind have experienced remarkable sensations from touching and petting them or putting their arms around their necks.

These experiences taught us that, regardless of people's circumstances, horses can be brought into their lives. Since we can communicate with horses in a multitude of ways—mentally, physically, and through extrasensory perception, visualization and telepathy—these alternative avenues work. Other authors and experts agree that the keen extrasensory abilities of horses make their healing powers nonlocal. Good trainers take this for granted and know that training continues in or out of the saddle, even during sleep and in dreams.

Margaret, a middle-aged woman taking lessons, said she had very deep and intimate conversations with her favorite gelding, Fredrico, while away from the ranch. The more they conversed and became familiar, the more relaxed she became. As Fredrico appeared more and more in her thoughts and fantasies, she found herself riding him mentally during the week. She progressed rapidly because she practiced in her mind, at home. Margaret found that as she became more simpatico with the horse, her own ability to intuit and visualize also grew.

We cannot stress enough that any true involvement with horses of any type will give you insight. Watching training, if not actually doing it yourself, can be a real eye-opener. Training a horse is all patience and heart, not intellect or force. Understanding comes from the heart, not the head. Training becomes a test for the trainer and in reality reveals more about the trainer than the horse. If we want to learn about our dark side, this is the test. Faced with challenges from the horse, we can see the imbalances in our dark and light natures. When we are tested, tried, humiliated, cajoled, what is our reaction? Do we become forgiving, patient and loving, or pompous, vengeful, weak and ineffectual? Whatever lurks inside always rears its ugly head. One trainer we encountered was so afraid of the horse's spirit and energy that he trained him to go backward instead of forward. Whenever the horse started to move ahead freely, he was taught to back up or stop. The result was a horse that push-pulled. He could never go forward without going back, nor could he move freely without thinking he should stop. The horse became confused and nervous because whatever he did was never "right." This particular trainer had a preoccupation with submission and dominance, indicative of a severe need to control. By contrast, some of the most artistic and talented trainers value a philosophy of interrelatedness and mutual respect. They first command respect by gaining the horse's attention. Teamwork and harmony are the basis of this method, and under these circumstances the horse becomes a willing partner and gives all. In observing training it is obvious how the trainer designs the horse's future. We do the same in our own lives.

The Horse Metaphor

Humans experience transitions in their lives. None of us are immune from these passages. Besides the milestones, enduring tragedy and coping with crises are features of living we all share in common. We have found that having a tangible metaphor, a living myth, helps us make the leaps of faith necessary to cope. With such myths, human trials can be less traumatic, and even amusing. The horse metaphor serves as a focal point to keep us centered and on track. By entering the world of natural instinct, we learn in an experiential way to judge for ourselves when we are straying too far. It offers us a yardstick to measure when our values are unnatural or too intellectual.

Most important, the metaphor shifts our attention from ourselves and solidifies an I-Thou orientation. Martin Buber developed this concept from a relationship he had with a horse he befriended in his youth. Branching out prevents us from becoming species-centric, thus increasing our empathy with the greater universe. Simply focusing our attention on ourselves and our problems to the exclusion of everything else reinforces our modern plague, narcissism. The horse liberates us from the confines of our ascribed roles because it is both fact and fiction. Through our identification with a horse we can learn about the natural and supernatural.

Working with horses has made it easier for us to handle life in general: stress, crises, death, terminal illnesses, vulnerabilities and a host of other trials. It has taught us to be more open, more malleable, and to approach life with a sense of adventure. We have also noticed that horses bring people together. They seem to know whom to bring into your life at the right moment, cementing relationships in a very profound way. Entering the world of the Classic Horse builds bridges between people of different cultures, religions and races, like a large extended family. The Equine Experience serves as a universal language, leading to new forms of dialogue, understanding and compassion. It takes work and love, but we can reach new heights of self-awareness and feelings by interacting with the

Classic Horse, in the saddle or out. As you read this book, see what the horse archetype stimulates in you. By understanding its nature, you will better understand your own.

2 Our Connection with Animals

What will it mean for the human race
if children come of age in a world bereft of
other living creatures? Their growing years
will be immeasurably less vivid and vibrant.
Their connection with the Earth will be severed,
and part of their inborn potential for amazement
will go uncultivated. It is not just that animals
make the world more scenic or picturesque.
The lives of animals are woven into our very
being—closer than our own breathing—
and our soul will suffer when they are gone.

—Gary Kowalski, *Do Animals Have Souls?*

Throughout the millennia, humans have sensed and respected the power of animal instinct; many ancient peoples held animals as sacred, as some current cultures still do. Within this context, it isn't difficult to understand our personification of other species. Our relationship with animals is deeper than mere interaction and involves mutual respect and many forms of symbiosis.

In ancient Greece, India, Spain, Persia and Egypt, animals were intimately woven into the fabric of everyday life. In agricultural communities, oxen increased the farmer's harvest, and horses revolutionized military defense for reigning powers. In homes, human babies were suckled on the milk of mares, ewes and goats, and, of course, animals have always provided resources for basic clothing, food and shelter everywhere. Horses were an integral part of Indo-European societies' expansion.

To keep their communities sanitary, many villages took advantage of dogs' natural scavenging tendencies. Egyptians recognized canines as valuable sentries. They bred the beautiful pharaoh hounds that were entrusted with guarding the pharaohs' tombs, thereby ensuring an undisturbed journey to the afterlife.

In the 1600s, Europeans condemned cats as diabolical and launched a campaign to eradicate them entirely. Not long after this, their efforts were rewarded with the devastating visitation of the bubonic plague. Only long after the European population was decimated did people realize that this misery was in large part self-inflicted, for they had killed the cats that ate the rats. The Cult of the Cat in ancient Egypt placed strict taboos on killing these sacred animals. The Egyptians were wise enough to realize that the cats controlled the rat population in the granaries.

From us, domesticated animals have received shelter, food and companionship. On balance, humans have probably benefited far more from animals than animals have from humans. We've certainly had a far more negative effect on other species and their environments than they have had on us. Although we have taken pride in our successful domestication of some species, researchers now contend that at least some, notably the canines, domesticated themselves in order to survive human incursion.

Animals and the Human Spirit

In addition to, or probably as a result of, their functional status for humans, animals have been incorporated into the spiritual/religious life of almost every society.

The bull played a major cultural and religious role in Minoan and Cretan civilizations. Participants in the Cult of the Bull used the animal in their rituals. Spanish bullfighting is a remnant of this tradition. The matador, adorned in a suit of light representing purity, faces the bull, a symbol of base instinct and carnal desire. In conquering the bull, matadors increase their own spiritual strength.

The minotaurs, fawns, centaurs, furry-footed trolls, mermaids and angels that have sprung from the oral tradition of so many cultures are part human, part beast. These mythical hybrids inhabit multiple realms, having some commerce with humans but always as a means of helping them enter the world of spirits, magic and the possibility of transformation.

In an animistic world view, every material manifestation of the universe has a soul. Everything around us, animate and inanimate, is listening, seeing, feeling and thinking. Within this paradigm, animals occupy a central role in our lives and our interactions with them acquire greater significance. A one-sided or hierarchical dynamic gives way to reciprocity between ourselves and other species.

Across diverse cultures, animals have played a key role in accompanying humans on psychological and spiritual quests. In myth and legend, they help their human brethren navigate through the obstacles of the unconscious to reach new heights of awareness. They are also seen as teachers, initiating people into the world of instinct and helping them transmute their ignobility into positive strengths.

The rich and complex symbolism of the horse in human history echoes within us on many levels. The very presence of the horse seems to evoke mythical themes for people. In literature and myth, horses reflect the powerful role they play in our unconscious. In fable and legend, they have attained mythic status. Often, they're portrayed as loyal protectors who, using telepathic and prophetic powers, warn their masters of impending difficulties.

Paul, a former client, had been the victim of a stabbing. Prior to this tragedy he had been a successful stockbroker. Since the crime he was plagued by anxiety and unable to sleep or concentrate. He was feeling helpless and impotent in every aspect of his life. Talking didn't seem to help him. In fact, remembering caused him more suffering. At this point in our careers we were not involved with horses except in a personal way, and we never mentioned this to Paul.

Several months into his therapy, Paul brought in a dream. In the dream a magnificent black stallion saved him from men dressed in black who were trying to hurt him. In exploring the significance of this dream, what struck Paul more than anything else was that he had not thought of horses since childhood. This dream triggered many old and comforting feelings for him. Unknown to us, he had always had a love for horses but never knew why. This dream stirred something inside of him that led to the strength he needed to function.

The following story was told to us by one of our dear friends, a social worker, who has worked with many dying people. Sylvia, her client, lay on her deathbed, and right before she died she turned to our friend and said, "I am ready to go. I see the white horse."

To the ancient Celts, horses were sacred creatures associated with the life cycle, power, fertility, physical and metaphysical travel, and good fortune. They believed the horse goddess was responsible for transporting the human soul into and out of its earthly existence at the appropriate season of life.

The horse embodied the sacredness of Earth and seasonal change. The Celts revered the white goddess mare Epona as a great queen. The fertility cult of Epona reached from Spain to eastern Europe and from northern Italy to Britain. As late as the 11th century, Irish kings were ritualistically united with this horse goddess.

Saint Francis, unlike his contemporaries in the Catholic church, unified the world of animals within himself. While

Francis was a Western Christian, his sensitivity to and affinity with all creation was in perfect accord with the theology of the Christian East, which holds creation as a unified whole. Saint Francis believed that animals are our connection to the divine on Earth—numinous messengers of God who perform a role similar to that of angels.

Carl Jung contended that wild horses represent the uncontrollable instinctual urges that erupt from our unconscious, even though we try to repress them. The fabled centaur that is half-man, half-horse represents an attempt to resolve this inner division and integrate our human and nonhuman sides. Jung saw the horse as a symbol of our base instincts and a symbol of water—the most life-sustaining substance. He also felt that horses in myth express the magical side of us, the mother within who is intuitive and understanding.

Jung saw animals as the epitome of true devotion in that they don't deviate from how God intended them to be—unlike their human counterparts, who tend to wander and rebel. Jung also felt that the animals that appear in our dreams act as divine emissaries who are there to guide us through our difficulties.

In his book *Mystical Christianity*, Jungian analyst John Sanford emphasizes the place animals occupy in our soul development: "They play a positive role in the psyche, and how we relate to them shows how related we are to the Self. That Jesus was related to the animal kingdom is shown in the Gospel of Mark, where we are told that after the temptations in the wilderness by Satan, Jesus was ministered to by the angels and the wild animals."[1]

Only in modern times have animals been physically and spiritually segregated from humans. Apart from their role as food and leather and as research subjects, animals are largely thought of as superfluous pets, with little to contribute.

It is also fascinating to note that a tendency to objectify horses throughout history has usually coincided with cultural periods when enlightenment and spirituality were at an ebb. By contrast, reverence, admiration and deep appreciation for horses usually signals a reemerging cultural and spiritual renaissance. Like fine wine, art and music, a passion for horses has often ushered in a revival of the sacred esthetic traditions.

As members of the Kingdom Animalia, humans share more than just an environment with other species. We share some evolutionary heritage as well. Biologists once taught that "ontogeny recapitulates phylogeny," which means that the progression of human (and nonhuman) life *in utero* mimics evolutionary development. Thus, during various developmental phases, we have ancestral structures like tails, gills and flippers. These are eventually absorbed or transformed into other organs or limbs so that they are absent in the newborn baby, but they are reminders of the common ground we share with our distant and not-so-distant relatives.

Although humans have one of the most highly developed cerebral cortices in the animal kingdom, deeper neural layers, like our "reptilian brain," roughly correspond structurally and functionally to neural tissues in other species. So there is a physiological basis for our identification and feeling of kinship with other animals.

Most Native American cultures have a strong animistic tradition. Animals may serve a community or individual totems. Totem animals are called upon to befriend, protect, inspire and heal. In the case of shamans, totem animals guide their human associates through unseen worlds. In tribal cultures all over the world, people believe strongly that each of us comes into the world under the stewardship of a specific animal that confers its own characteristic strengths upon its human charge. The astrological systems of India and China are based on similar human-animal associations.

Selecting a personal totem is a serious task. Individuals must decide which aspect(s) of their personality they want to enhance. To find a proper match, it's critical that each person understand the animal's essential nature because for better or worse, communion with a chosen totem will bring about a transfer of energy from animal to person.

In a variety of cultures throughout the world, people know that animals are endowed with concentrated energies that mirror those existing in the larger universe. Some animals, among them horses, maintain a balance of yin and yang ener-gies. Others, like lions and deer, possess a larger complement of one particular energy.

There is no such thing as a "bad" totem animal, but there are poor choices for any given individual. For example, a very aggressive person would want to avoid choosing a strong predator as his or her totem. The right animal selected will, through its own example, help the person correct energy imbalances and attain wholeness.

Animistic relationships are especially potent because they transcend the physical dimension. As the animal-human interchange deepens, some change actually occurs at an atomic or subatomic level through the catalyst of intense feelings (a manifestation of energy). The magic of this chemistry opens the individual, allowing incorporation of the animal's spiritual essence. This pulsating interchange is our tie to the cosmos.

This connection has its roots in early psychology, in the work of Franz Mesmer in the late 18th century. Mesmer was fascinated with the Greeks' ideas about magnetism, a physical energy involving positive and negative charge. Paracelsus reportedly cured illnesses by arousing this energy. In conducting his own experiments, Mesmer came to the conclusion that living matter is influenced by earthly and celestial forces that he collectively called "animal magnetism." His discovery prompted him to develop a specific technique to invoke this energy, which he assumed was buried deeply within our unconscious. The resulting method was called mesmerism, the precursor to hypnosis. Then, as now, Mesmer's ideas were the subject of much controversy and were met with strong resistance within scientific circles.

When tapped, this energy, friction or animal magnetism not only cures mental and physical disease but can mean the difference between success and failure in life. The most successful people in any field possess a certain indefinable "quality X." In spite of all the books written on success and how to achieve it, very few explore the intangible characteristics of those who manage to "catch fire."

A familiar example of quality X at work can be seen in the theater. Great actors and actresses exude a certain magnetism or charisma that completely captivates an audience. When a performer successfully draws on this, the audience feels an indescribable attraction and intense involvement. The renowned drama teacher Constantin Stanislavski knew that an actor either had this quality or didn't. He described the quality as "an indefinable, intangible quality; it is the inexplicable charm of an actor's whole being; it transforms even his deficiencies into assets. His idiosyncrasies and shortcomings become things to be copied by his admirers."[2] On stage, this quality takes on a life of its own and gives rise to true art.

True Intimacy

In our work, we turn to animals, rather than to people, as sources of this alchemical, transforming energy. Generally speaking, our needs and expectations cloud our communications with each other and preclude relating at a deep enough level. Consciously or unconsciously, we manipulate each other, and this gives rise to struggles with power, control, projection and idealization. These are all natural aspects of our humanness.

In relating to animals, most of the communication patterns we maintain in relationships with other people are inappropriate and futile. Because they are blissfully free of ego and all the psychological machinations it gives rise to, animals respond to what's beneath the surface. We can't disguise our feelings from animals because we give off telling cues, including movement and smell, that convey our true state. Feelings bring about chemical changes, some of which result in release of pheromones. Animals smell our fear, anger, contentment, et cetera. To establish trust with animals, we have to base our interactions on honesty, mutual respect and compassion. If we don't, they'll know it and respond accordingly.

Intimacy must always have true friendship as its foundation. With this basis, the relationship is lasting because it emanates from the heart. Participants in this kind of intimacy appear to be connected by an invisible thread that has the potential to bind them together even after death, from one incarnation to the next.

Animals teach us how to love spiritually. Their feelings for one another are not only touching but enviable in their strength and depth. Through their example, we can learn to deepen our sensitivity and humanity. The act of gentling an animal is not a one-way exchange but a mutual process whereby we also gentle ourselves.

Belonging

Because we design our own personalities, it's important to know what it is that we love. It forms the essence of our personalities. The people and things we become attached to, consciously or unconsciously, help mold our character. By the same token, the things that we loathe shape us as well, through our very rejection of them. Throughout life, we develop our own individual tastes. To understand ourselves and others, we need to be aware of what they are.

People feel very definite affinities and aversions toward certain animals. These feelings are not frivolous but reflect heartfelt ideals. If you were to ask your friends which animal they felt an affinity for, you'd find among them dog people, cat people, rat people, frog people, pig people, horse people, and so on. If you explored more deeply, you would discover that the animals these individuals are drawn to have qualities that they strive to attain or that symbolically represent something they want to become. People who love all animals equally have probably managed to reconcile the multiple and often conflicting facets of human nature within themselves.

To understand our own character, it's important to know "where we live" psychosocially. For instance, which instincts do we cultivate and which do we allow to atrophy? Compared with other members of the animal kingdom, humans largely lack true instincts. Instead, we're characterized (by ourselves, of course) by a high degree of behavioral plasticity. Humans also have instincts, though they are probably so deeply woven into the fabric of our beings that we can't see them any more clearly than we can see the bridge of our own nose. We are, however, capable of displaying a wider range of behavior in a given situation than most other animals. For example, while certain other social species have herd, flock or pack instincts, humans can manifest aspects of any or all of these tendencies. It's useful to examine and compare social instincts in other species to see where humans fall with respect to our level of social development. This exercise can broaden our perspective on relatedness. It can also provide insights into potential strategies for working with individuals and groups, whether in your own personal life, in your business, or in confronting day-to-day crises.

All of the strategies described on the following pages are species' ways of coping given the environment in which they evolved. We are not making any value judgments regarding the relative "goodness" of these separate behaviors, each of which works well for the species that use it.

The Herd Instinct

Horses are social animals with strong herd instincts. They live in close groupings because they crave companionship above all else. Anyone who has gone out trail riding in a group knows that it's almost impossible to keep a horse separated from the other horses for very long. Domesticated horses become extremely attached to people who care for and are kind to them and generally treat them as members of their own herd.

When a horse is isolated or otherwise deprived of companionship, it becomes depressed. If, on the other hand, it's allowed to express its own nature within its community, whether its members are horses or humans, it will maintain a playful, lively spirit. If a horse suffers from a severe loss or trauma, it can undergo a psychological breakdown akin to that seen in humans who have endured a comparable trauma.

Herd animals like the horse are not blind followers. Although social by nature, each member of the herd retains its own individuality, fulfilling a distinct function and occupying a defined position in the group hierarchy. A horse raised within the context of its herd knows the consensual communication signals so vital to its own well-being, as well as that of the larger group. If a horse ranks number 10 in a herd of 10 horses, it is nevertheless content. Uncertainty as to its position within the herd would be far more distressing than simply having a low ranking.

Developmentally, young horses follow roughly the same line as human infants, although they're born more precocious and development is comparatively compressed in time. An early phase of relative dependency leads to mature individuation within an interdependent group. Mares and foals form strong attachment bonds. The mare will go to great lengths to protect her baby from hunters.

Horse herds are highly developed social systems with strict codes of behavior, taboos, customs and rules that ensure cohesion, organization and survival. All members of the herd depend on the lead mare to guide them away from danger and toward life's necessities. The stallion drives the herd from behind, watching for stragglers and fending off potential predators. If it's necessary for the safety of the larger group, the stallion will actually kill herd members that are too weak to keep up. The lead mare and stallion work cooperatively as a team, balanced and equal in their leadership roles.

The Flock Instinct

People with a sheep or flock mentality find it difficult, if not impossible, to change. Domestic sheep epitomize the flock animal. They are quite docile, but nearly totally oblivious to what's going on around them. Left to their own devices and without a shepherd, they can be destructive to the environment and to themselves (this is probably not true of wild sheep), wandering about with no sense of direction or purpose. Sheep browse constantly and rarely look up. Other than a thick coat and whatever safety can be had in numbers, they have no protective mechanisms and are easily picked off by predators.

Anyone who has watched sheep for a time will notice that they seem to have no true attachment to each other. Their togetherness appears to be motivated by a need to huddle rather than a need to interact. Even when the ewes lamb, their behavior doesn't change significantly.

Although one sees some variation among individuals, bonding between the female and her offspring isn't highly developed as it is in many other mammals. The intensity of maternal drive seems to be a function of the mother's basic disposition and previous mothering experience. We've witnessed ewes walk off soon after giving birth, leaving a bawling lamb wet with afterbirth and unattended on the ground. Some mothers actually run from their newborns, while others simply stand and stare quizzically at the lamb. A coyote can sneak among sheep at night and kill a lamb without rousing other sheep, including a lamb's mother.

The Pack Instinct

Coyotes and wolves are pack animals that band together for breeding and hunting. Hunting cooperatively gives them courage and optimizes their chances of a successful kill.

Cultures in which humans once coexisted with wolves have proper names such as Wölfgang and Lupe that translate to "wolf" or "she-wolf." Robert Eisler felt that this wolf naming, which occurs in many languages, clearly suggests that the transition of humans from scavenger-gatherers to hunter-gatherers was a conscious one and that it was accompanied by a deep-seated emotional shift that remains a part of our unconscious, or what Jung called our "collective unconscious." Humans identify with the predator and identify themselves as predators.

The werewolf myth, the transmogrification from human into predatory beast, may have its origins here as well. The clinical term "lycanthropy" is described by Eisler in his book *Man into Wolf* as a "form of raving madness manifesting itself in the patient's belief that he is a wolf, with lupine teeth, refusing to eat anything but raw, bloody meat, emitting bestial howls and indulging in unrestrained sexual attacks on any victim he can overpower."[3]

Around the time of the Second World War, Adolf Hitler revived the werewolf legend in his prized paramilitary group, Organization Werewolf. The name was borrowed from a 1920s terrorist gang that had cultivated a reputation as a demonic wolf pack that hunted down its victims under the dark cloak of night.

The age-old myths about the wolf and its behavior, as it turns out, have little bearing on reality. We now know that the wolf has been unjustly demonized and accounts of its viciousness far overstated. Like horses, wolves band together for companionship and maintain a tight, hierarchical social structure. Wolves also bond closely with one another and mourn when they lose a pack member. The grieving period may last several weeks, during which rambunctious play stops and individual wolves occasionally let out a sorrowful howl.

Human Urges

In trying to bring about a transfiguration of untamed human urges, timing is critical. Once a youth is swept away by blood-lust and immediate sexual gratification, the potential for change significantly diminishes. To diffuse these preoccupations, authority figures need to challenge our youth early on and in creative ways.

Examining different animals' social behavior in groups can help us become aware of our own inner (instinctive) affiliations and styles of communicating. We can use the dynamic interplay between herds, flocks and packs as a model for sorting out and solving our own difficult dynamics. For example, we can ask, "What is my orientation here?" and "Do I identify with the herd, the flock or the pack? What about the people around me? Where do they fit in?" Acting out these various roles can prove enlightening.

We've noticed that today fewer people display a herd-type orientation to life. Instead, what we see more of is the relationship of predator/prey. This serious social imbalance is characterized by a cat-and-mouse dynamic, which is one reason criminal activity has become an increasingly prevalent pastime. To restore a sense of order and safety within our communities, we need to correct our direction and regain equilibrium.

In nonthreatening situations, a horse is capable of showing great affection and love. The horse shifts to aggression when confronted by an aggressor, then reverts to a basically loving nature when there is no danger present. A horse is capable of drawing upon both sides of its nature.

Unfortunately, humans have not developed the facility to shift between these two energies, nor have we made a concerted effort to hone our powers of perception. Consequently, we tend to operate through life on "automatic pilot." In our state of blunted awareness, we behave something like sheep. We fail to see what goes on around us, or we deny what we see.

The mistrust we have in our intuitive abilities leaves us, like sheep, extremely vulnerable. Our culture's present emphasis on the importance of intellect at the expense of instinctual knowing has rendered us defenseless. We have crippled ourselves in our hesitation to mobilize our instincts, even when to do so would save our lives. We treat our instincts like vestigial appendages we no longer need, and instead we think, ponder, analyze and criticize. By the time we've thought things through and are ready to act, our enemy has cut us out of the flock as the next victim. Our hyper-rationalism hurts us by limiting our spontaneity and ability to respond from instinct when necessary. Detached from our most valuable clues, we are becoming increasingly disoriented. As a result, our feelings of helplessness mount.

Awareness of these group behavior patterns of affiliation gives us a choice. When we think in these terms while considering current personal and social problems—particularly violence—things become clearer. It makes us conscious of the unconscious dynamics we may be acting out. Many doors to self-improvement will open if we have a chance to explore and master our instincts.

To realize the growth-promoting value of our instincts, we needed a safe context within which to work with them. We found such a context in the horse arena.

3

The Healing Horse

Every moment and every event of every man's life on Earth plants something in his soul. For just as the wind carries thousands of winged seeds, so each moment brings with it germs of spiritual vitality in the minds and wills of men.

—Thomas Merton,
New Seeds of Contemplation

We first used horses in our clinical work years ago with a client named John who was referred to us after innumerable hospitalizations. John was diagnosed as schizophrenic when he was a child, and his symptoms had become so severe that he was on his way to becoming a forgotten human being.

At this advanced phase of schizophrenia, John, who was only in his early 20s, had lost hope and was resigned to a life of mental illness. He was convinced he had no purpose, that he was a burden to others and that suicide was the only option available. John's despair was so pervasive we could feel it when we entered his room, and his posture reflected the emotional weight he carried.

Because people avoided him, John began to feel contaminated. He was sure his disease was contagious and infecting those he contacted. The hospital staff that had poured so much time and care into working with him over several years was understandably demoralized over his lack of progress. It seemed that at 22 years of age, John was destined to become a chronic patient, living his life in and out of institutions.

As a therapist, when you accept a patient like John into your care, you begin to wonder all kinds of things about yourself. We wondered if we were deluding ourselves in trying to effect recovery in someone who was as far gone as John appeared to be, but we've always erred on the side of optimism, even against heavy odds. One of our greatest strengths is plain old fortitude. We have found that, so far, this works well for us personally and professionally.

When he first came to us, John was virtually mute and, when he did vocalize, his speech was unintelligible. He had no friends, his family had abandoned him, and he was obviously used to being utterly alone. Suffering from a constant and debilitating depression, he spent most of his time lying in bed, responding to auditory hallucinations. In addition to his other symptoms, John liked to cut himself. We sensed that his depression caused him to feel deadened and that he mutilated himself as a means of feeling something—even if it was pain—that would make him feel alive.

Knowing where to begin treatment with John was a challenge. He didn't talk to anyone but his imaginary friends, who consisted mostly of dead rock musicians. During these exchanges, we were totally invisible to him. He much preferred their company to ours. Over the years, he had learned that we mortals had little to offer him.

Sitting with John day after day, unacknowledged and unappreciated, we began to feel like outsiders. As our feelings of alienation grew, we told John that we felt left out. For John, this represented a new perspective and a large role reversal. It had never occurred to him that someone might feel excluded in his presence, when he himself had spent his entire life feeling like an outcast.

Our refusal to let John ignore us triggered his curiosity. This is the point at which professional distance is so vital to success in therapy. A "detached involvement" with clients allows us to interact fully with them without taking on, or otherwise trying to get rid of, their pain. If there is any hope for change through therapy, clients must feel their own feelings, including pain. The key to engaging John's attention was to tell him the truth about what we saw and felt in the very moment. This was a new experience for him, since he had been accustomed to hospital staff being especially careful around him.

We were determined to respect John and treat him with dignity. Never did we baby or feel sorry for him. Rather than playing to his weaknesses, we sided with his strengths. Initially, John didn't like being treated as someone other than a helpless, hopeless patient, but as therapists we've observed that being crazy over an extended period is sometimes a career choice—a debilitating luxury we'd rather not support.

We never tried to talk him out of suicide; we simply offered the truth that we would miss him. We also tried to help him think through the potential results of this act. Would his problems really be solved with death? We felt that, more than anything else, John needed friendship, understanding and opportunities.

He soon found our interactive style engaging and began to acknowledge us. Understanding his personal struggle, accepting him as a multifaceted person, and dealing with him truthfully and directly helped John to begin rebuilding a shattered psyche and to renew his spirit.

As John began to spend less time in fantasy, he noticed that he had become bored with his problems and needed to be more productive. This was a good sign. As he regained his sanity he became painfully aware of his alienation and loneliness. After spending years in and out of institutions, John felt a bit like Rip Van Winkle, awakening to a changed world after a long sleep.

Overcoming his estrangement from others was a major component of John's full and lasting recovery. Like all of us, to reconstruct his life he needed to be involved in something besides thinking about his problems. To give him something to take charge of and thereby build his confidence, we assigned him to work with our Welsh pony, Cricket. John began to learn everything there is to know about horses: cleaning stalls, grooming, handling tack, riding, nutrition and health care.

Cricket was a very trustworthy and gentle animal—perfect for the novice equestrian. Over the next year, as John came faithfully every weekend to care for the pony, his handling skills grew and his relationship with Cricket blossomed. Eventually, he became accomplished enough to ride the local trails. On these outings, he would meet and speak to other riders on the path. Through these brief exchanges, John realized that he shared a common interest with these people and that he had something to say.

John began to think of himself as a person and a horseman, whereas prior to this breakthrough his only identity had been that of a schizophrenic. He had found his vehicle to the outside world. One day he proudly announced to us that he'd found a job at an event center. When we asked what he'd said in his interview, he replied, "They asked me if I had any experience with horses, and I said 'Yes!'" John held that job for 20 years. After retiring from a supervisory position, he pursued a lifelong dream: he returned to college and earned his degree in English. In his recovery, John had far exceeded his and our wildest dreams. We never imagined that a young man so damaged would end up teaching us as much about life as John did.

We had always felt horses were special companions. After seeing John's transformation, we started seeing them in another light—as potent agents of change. We began to think about developing a treatment method using horses as our confederates, but didn't act on it for several more years. At the time, we were still sticking to professional conventions. While we thought the horses might be great for patients, we were unaware of how good they would be for us, too.

To the Country

It was difficult to imagine abandoning our training institute in San Francisco, but the idea of moving to the country and exploring the use of horses as healing agents stayed with us. We had been pushed into rethinking many of our notions about healing. Even more important, we were pushed into rethinking many of our notions about life.

We were always intrigued by the concept of healing environments. The activities, people and settings we choose all comprise a milieu that we naturally internalize. What we experience within our milieu generates a store of memories and over time informs our core self. The environments in which we live, work and play shape our attitudes and personalities. The powerful influence of surroundings is frequently overlooked.

Some environments are healing, while others are stagnant or even toxic. This is especially noticeable in treatment settings for severely ill individuals. Such patients virtually absorb the objects and events around them. (Children also do this, but the phenomenon is age-specific and appropriate for them.) For example, if a room is completely unstimulating, a psychotic patient may see everyone in it as literally dead. Conversely, if the room is visually and otherwise vibrant, the patient may instead see rainbows stretching across the room.

This wholesale internalizing of the environment is painful and disruptive for psychotic patients and leaves them feeling vulnerable to the vagaries of the world around them. Although the average person doesn't experience these extremes, everyone does experience the same phenomenon, only to a much lesser extent. Normally, we filter environmental stimuli to varying degrees so that we have a sense of boundaries between ourselves and everything around us. We all know what it's like to have our own mood altered by being with a friend who is in the throes of grief or joy or another strong feeling. Something as simple as the color of a room or the level of ambient light affects us. Whether we're aware of it or not, we are all susceptible to our changing environments.

Much applied research has been done on how the environment affects everything from learning to mood. During a vacation in Switzerland, we visited a therapeutic community for mentally ill patients. The residents lived on and ran this fully operative farm. They thrived in this atmosphere. The recovery rate there was high and the recidivism rate low.

Because of their heightened state of sensitivity, psychotic people can teach us many things. Their idiosyncratic world view often provides them with some astute insights. Like children, they have access to some truths that the rest of us have forgotten. Working with these people can be quite enlightening.

We asked some of our psychotic patients what they would choose if they could choose an ideal place for themselves to heal. They were unanimous in selecting a place in the country where animals are present. They described urban life as chaotic, unnatural and uncomfortable. Some reported that their delusions and hallucinations quiet down, their sleep becomes more restful, and they're less prone to having nightmares when they're in natural surroundings. Many patients remembered that in some of their bleakest moments they had found solace in a pet. As one young man said, "When I had no one to turn to I could confide in my cat. Animals saved me by connecting me to life." These sentiments mirror many of our own beliefs about what constitutes a healing environment.

In 1981, we moved ourselves and our practice to the country, opened residential treatment facilities, and developed our equine therapy program. A quiet, remote country setting would afford clients who were in transition a sanctuary in which they could venture inward safely. We ourselves were also searching for an alternative to the prevailing mentality in the urban setting.

To maximize and intensify our clients' self-exploration, we enlisted horses as therapeutic guides. We wanted to go beyond an analytical approach to therapy and fully engage our clients—body and soul. The horses also facilitated our becoming fully involved in the clients' processes while maintaining the professional awareness and distance so vital for perspective.

Equine Therapy

Our goal was to help people go beyond where conventional therapies often leave them. For some, conventional therapy doesn't work at all. Others manage, through much hard work, to develop greater awareness of their problems but fail to construct a new life or enhance their present one.

It's like spending endless hours preparing the soil for a vegetable garden and neglecting to plant the seeds. Without working through the last critical phase, they're likely to revert to habitual behaviors. It's also true that people today have begun to tire of therapy. They're burnt out on the jargon, the predictable lines of investigation, not to mention the time and expense that must be invested. We wanted the people with whom we worked to experience not just better functioning but joy in their lives. We wanted to get them to live life rather than to dissect it ad nauseum.

We saw equine therapy as a way not only to bring problems to the surface and resolve them but to help people find greater fulfillment and wholeness. Working with horses would naturally bring instincts into play. Because of certain characteristics horses and people share—for instance, the need for strong bonding within a well-defined community—we felt the horses could strike a reparative chord in the human psyche. Horses represent what we hoped to achieve through therapy—an individual capable of establishing close bonds within a cohesive social group and a path toward restoring humanity, toward healthy membership within our human "herd."

Horses very naturally express basic instincts necessary to the physical, psychological and spiritual survival of humans. Working with horses gives people a concrete, external way to master aspects of themselves that frighten them most, like sex- and aggression-related behavior. As clients learn to handle a horse and channel the animal's drives, they spontaneously internalize the process. Through unconsciously identifying with the horses, individuals come to understand their own basic drives and the value of developing self-control. Working with a horse, they gain a new sense of self-mastery.

Riding, itself, is only one component of our work. We stress the importance of all aspects of the relationship with the horse. Each program participant learns gentling, training, grooming, nutrition, showing, handling a horse at liberty, et cetera. If a client chooses not to participate, in some way or at all, we work with that nonparticipation.

Some clients choose (and are free) to just sit and observe. We've always maintained a strict policy of noninterference in this regard because we've seen that each participant's unique pace and direction reveal themselves if given patience and time. Depending on what is best for the client at a particular time, we may elect to work in a group setting or in individual sessions.

Although our first clients in equine therapy consisted of juveniles or adults with emotional or behavioral problems, we later started including street-gang members and substance abusers. As word got out about what we were doing, people seeking to simply improve the quality of their daily lives began approaching us for help. These included families interested in more and better communication, business executives wanting to sharpen their leadership and team-building skills, busy people needing to reduce stress in their lives, and spiritual seekers.

We have tried using several breeds of horses with our clients but discovered that almost all were too difficult to work with for one reason or another. We researched and found that Iberian (Spanish) horses were bred for centuries for their excellent minds and their interactive contact with people and their families who raise them. Many of the other breeds were used for other reasons, such as war and farming. The Spanish horses we selected to work with—the Peruvian breed—have gentle, consistent and trustworthy dispositions.

These qualities are not limited to a few exceptional horses but are characteristic of the breed. Peruvians have other appealing qualities, including an extremely smooth gait, which makes riding bounce-free and easier for riders of all levels. An intelligent, gentle breed, they have been developed over the centuries as a trustworthy family horse. They are also known for their responsiveness. Physical force is not necessary to ride or control them.

Master trainer Jean-Philippe Giacomini describes the characteristics selected for Iberians.

The horse must be strong enough to carry the rider easily, resistant enough to cover long distances at speed and work with a high degree of energy for a long time, as in the bullfight or in a three-day event. He must be very brave so as not to mind when he occasionally gets hurt by a bull or an obstacle or gets threatened by another horse/rider combination like in polo, horseball, et cetera. He needs to be patient in order to tolerate incessant demands from the rider during the bullfight without becoming irritated, fearful or sullen. He must be extremely careful not to touch the poles of the show jumps and to stay away from the bull's horns, yet bold enough to jump fences willingly and to approach the bull with a daring courage. The Iberian's mind is in some ways similar to the one of a sheepdog, always eager to work, anxious to learn and quick to remember the exercises learned years earlier, seemingly without much prompting. Their degree of intelligence, developed by long selection, is very high, but does not bring them to boredom because it is combined with good will. Many school horses of this breed, after years of being ridden by beginners, still perform generously and correctly when asked. Their docility is exemplary and strong stallions can be seen ridden in company by children as young as six or seven, whom they obey purely out of gentility. The psychic qualities of this horse are as important if not more important than the physical ones. One of the particular abilities of the Iberian horse is to easily understand the 'difficulties' of high-level training. He seems never to get confused about the many different types of movements and situations. His quickness of mind has served him well; he is the circus horse of choice and practically has the monopoly on fancy movie work. Columella . . . says eulogistically: ". . . as to temperament, the most esteemed are those, which although easily excited, can nevertheless be calmed, and those which although calm are hard workers." This particularity of temperament is unique to Iberian horses. [1]

It is this constellation of qualities that makes the Iberian horse invaluable for working with people.

We envisioned the equine therapy program as much more than recreation. It was designed as a vehicle for personal adventure into the realms of mind, body and spirit. The horse is the guide for travel—external and internal. This forum lets us simultaneously work, love and play—a healing combination.

4

Riding Horses
to Health

Relationship is the mirror in which
the ways of our thinking are revealed.
In the facts of relationship lies truth, not
away from relationship. There is obviously
no such thing as living in isolation.
We may carefully cut off various forms
of physical relationship, but the
mind is still related.

—Krishnamurti,
On Mind and Thought

Our biological birth is a given, but our psychological and spiritual births are far more tenuous and challenging. To find inner peace and spiritual wealth we must begin with the assumption of basic unity. This is a springboard to successful maturation that helps us sustain our hope and optimism through the most difficult of life's trials.

In myth, this feeling of basic unity is known as paradise, a metaphor for a place within us where conflict ceases and perfect harmony exists. Paradise also symbolizes a bygone era when the division between humans and nature did not exist—a time when humans were more comfortable with themselves. Humans still have this sense of original harmony and unity in the womb. Growing up, we're left with an unconscious desire to recapture this lost feeling of oneness.

Relationships are the one vehicle we have to repair our separateness and regain a sense of communion. It's impossible to change ourselves in isolation. Because we see ourselves only through our own eyes, we develop a distorted concept of ourselves and the rest of creation. Our relationships can relieve these distortions and curb our tendencies to see ourselves as excessively good or bad (or both). The feedback we get from others, especially in close relationships, brings personal issues we need to explore to the forefront so we can examine them in full light. Because it is through relationships that we get to see who we truly are, we must work within that context if we want to change ourselves in any deep, fundamental way.

In order to maximize the transformational power of our interactions, it helps to occasionally return to the archetypal relationship of mother and child. A relationship dynamic that shares many characteristics of the early maternal environment supports deep self-exploration. In this context, our inner essence is unmasked, allowing access to our core self, even if it is deeply buried.

Bonding at this primal level can be a potent catalyst. When the foundation of the relationship is deep love and compassion, it can move us to heal. Loving rejuvenates the spirit and gives birth to the soul. This type of attachment is critical for all of us, through each and every life phase. But we're also keenly aware that establishing such a relationship is easier said than done. Trying to create one in a traditional therapeutic setting is too mechanistic and contrived an approach. After years of traditional psychotherapy, we found that its curative effects are short-lived and limiting to a client's sense of complete living.

The concept of love is elusive and, therefore, difficult to bring to life. There are as many definitions of love as there are people. We wanted to center our work around an activity that would recapture and revive the early bonding instinct in a simple, direct way, which is one of the primary reasons we thought of bringing in horses.

The attachment formed must be an authentic one in which feelings flow freely and spontaneously. Living among horses was a powerfully emotional experience that so permeated us, heart and soul, that we thought being around horses might have the same effect on others. Here, we felt, was a natural and safe way to establish a true and deep connection with another living being.

Many of the qualities inherent in the mother/infant interaction can easily be developed between a person and a horse. Through the horse, a maternal love is available and the relationship is uncomplicated by the expectations with which human interactions are charged. Yet because we're using animals as the source of this love, the human is less likely to become excessively dependent. Clients keep their power, identity and dignity while recapturing an element missing in their lives. This dynamic has a reparative effect on people and draws them out because it speaks to the heart rather than the intellect.

In most people, horses elicit some feeling reaction. With some individuals, the result is instant harmony, while with others it is discord. Although these responses seem antithetical, they're not. The antithesis is actually the absence of any feeling, in which case no healing can occur. Regardless of whether the feelings generated are negative or positive, the relationship is a healing one because of the presence of feeling itself. If individuals can be moved on a feeling level, they can gain access to their creative cores.

Horses have the uncanny ability to illuminate who we are and where we need to go. They respond to us as unique individuals and somehow understand who we are in our hearts and souls. Horses can touch deep recesses in us that are inaccessible to most people—regions people are afraid to address in others, much less in themselves. In addition to this revelatory quality, horses bring to relationships endless love and compassion. Dialogue becomes a prayer of God when the dialogue between the horse and rider is enacted in the heart.

The healing effect of horses is exemplified by our work with a schizophrenic young woman named Mary. When she came to our residential treatment program, she was actively hallucinating, cut off from the world and completely nonverbal. Although she was completely unresponsive to us at that time, we would sit and talk to her for extended periods, telling her fairy tales and stories.

This went on for almost a year. Mary's silence seemed like it would never end. For us, this was truly an exercise in patience and faith. At times, it took a lot of soul searching to continue. We became acutely aware of how impatient we humans can be. Mary's silence taught us how well we can come to know one another without words. The quiet tends to deepen our awareness and sensitivity.

When at last Mary began speaking, she told us about her world and the pain she endured. She believed she was destined to die a martyr and told us that she suffered from arrows piercing her sides and knives stabbing her chest.

When Mary went outside into the natural surroundings of the treatment facility grounds, she could only appreciate its possibilities as a setting for her own death. Each time she passed a lake on the property, she remarked how suitable a spot it would be for her drowning. For all the despairing quality of her comments, she was confiding in us, indicating that at least some seed of trust was growing. As Mary's treatment continued, we had to garner as much faith to treat her as she had to get well.

It was at this time that a fellow horse breeder approached us for help with an extremely dangerous horse he had just acquired named Indomable ("indomable" means "untamable" in Spanish). Indomable was a magnificent horse who had, unfortunately, been abused by his previous handlers. As a result of this, he stayed constantly fearful and trusted no one. Our breeder friend reasoned that because we'd had such success with our clients, we might be able to do something with horses as well.

When we hitched Indomable's rope to a pole, he was so upset that he pulled the entire pole out of the ground, complete with its concrete base. To work with him at all, we had to place him in a stall. There he adopted a defensive stance and maintained it, with his back to the door, head in the corner of the stall and ears cocked back. When he did glance back at us, fury and fear were evident in his eyes.

Mary had reached a point in her therapy where she had started to participate in the horse program and was having contact with the animals. One afternoon soon after Indomable's arrival, she came down to watch us work with him. The horse stood in his usual defensive posture. Mary surprised us by offering to intervene. "Let me help him," she suggested. "I think I know what's wrong with him."

As therapists, we're known as risk-takers, but we had to act responsibly and think this offer through. It was a difficult choice for us because we were scared to death she might be taking a ridiculous chance. On one hand, this reaching out might signify real progress for Mary. On the other hand, it might be a manifestation of a still-present suicidal urge. We wanted to be fair. We took a calculated risk and gave her the go-ahead, but stayed close by to make certain that a delicate and potentially dangerous situation didn't escalate into a tragedy.

We allowed Mary to stand at the entrance with the door

open behind her. She went in quietly and simply stayed still with the terrified horse. He watched her and snorted threateningly but made no move to hurt her. After that, she went into his stall every day. Sometimes she talked softly to him, while at other times they just stood together in silence. On occasion, he would look at but never move toward her. We simply stood back and let the process happen and kept our mouths shut (something that's very hard for us to do). Finally, after almost six months of this daily routine, Indomable inched his way over to Mary, sniffed her from head to toe, then retreated again, having frightened himself at coming so close.

The horse remained standoffish for several weeks more. Then, during one of their daily sessions, Indomable walked over to Mary and stood there, as though he were waiting for her to respond. As she reached out to him, she was overwhelmed by a feeling of closeness and kinship. On this day, Indomable did not retreat. Each day after that, he allowed her to come closer and closer for longer periods. Eventually, Mary was actually able to put a halter on him.

In describing what she believed happened between the two of them, she said, "I understood him because he was just like me. He was having the same problems I was having. I only did for him exactly what you did for me." This represented a huge step in Mary's progress toward health. The nurturing she provided Indomable consisted of a simple, empathic, listening presence combined with patience and a readiness to respond. Her ability to provide this nurturing to another meant she herself had deeply internalized this same process. Her understanding of it signified the presence of a new self-awareness.

Mary and Indomable, in their symbiosis, moved one another toward health. Mary completed her treatment program with us and now lives independently. Before she left us, she fulfilled one of her dreams—to ride her beloved Indomable. For his part, Indomable went on to become a responsive and wonderful show horse. The trust established in his relationship with Mary allowed him to trust others as well.

Horse Sense and Sensitivity

Sometimes social workers plead with us to accept into our program a child no one else wants to deal with because his/her behavior is so difficult to manage. If we get a good feeling about the child, we'll try, even if we're taking a huge risk. In making educated assessments, it's hard to know how much pain someone is in until he or she trusts you enough to let you know. In the beginning, we often feel as though we're working in the dark, hoping that if we hang in long enough, we will learn enough from the child to be able to help.

Horses are wonderful at discerning people's moods. We once worked with a 14-year-old, David, who had suffered from severe emotional illness for two years and had lost his desire to live. He had come to view death as a refuge. When he arrived at our facility and we introduced him to the horses, he was especially drawn to the stallion Trianero. These two ended up establishing a close connection. Being around the horses calmed David and provided a temporary respite from his internal turmoil. We were very grateful that Trianero could reach this boy when we could not.

The magnitude and constancy of David's pain were greater, though, than we suspected. One night, in a state of deep despair, David hid a piece of glass in his hand with the intention of going off and killing himself with it, but he had to stop at the corral first to say good-bye to his friend Trianero. He climbed over the fence and began telling the horse his woes, then opened his hand to reveal the piece of glass. Trianero butted the boy's hand with his head and knocked the glass from his palm. David dissolved into tears and ended up staying with the horse, crying himself to sleep in the corral. With the boy at his feet, Trianero stood watch like a sentinel. When dawn broke, it was not just a new day for David but the beginning of a new life. When we found him in the corral that morning, we were stunned at what had brought him there. We couldn't help but notice that life goes on with or without us. Somehow, nature takes its course.

Because Trianero provided a silent, nonmanipulative and nonjudgmental presence, David had been able to open up in his own way and reveal the extent of his inner suffering. Regardless of the horse's conscious or unconscious intent, the boy felt embraced by this safe presence in a way that he probably couldn't with people. This is not at all an uncommon phenomenon. Social workers and psychologists who bring companion animals into nursing homes as part of their work with the elderly report that nursing home residents who refuse to interact with any of the people around them spontaneously and immediately open up to the animals.

Horses seem to know what people really need. They ignore the outward form and respond, instead, to the person's inner substance. The mentally ill feel frightened of the world and of people. A horse, sensing this childlike vulnerability in a patient, typically slows down and softens its movements so as not to cause alarm.

Another of our clients was a 12-year-old girl who had been abandoned by her parents when she was two years old. Sally had spent her life in institutions. In addition to feeling rejected and unwanted, she hallucinated and wet her bed regularly—something that made her feel very ashamed. The freckle-faced girl was attractive, although she wasn't aware of it. She hated her hair because her peers had ridiculed her all through her childhood for her flaming red mane.

Sally had the habit of repeating everything she heard people say. This upset other children in her company, who teased her about it as incessantly as she echoed them. Sally had been picked on a lot in her short life and was understandably sensitive to ridicule. When she felt pushed beyond her limit, she would blow up in anger, scratch the other kids with her fingernails, or flail at them with a stick or other object.

Keeping peace between Sally and the other residents threatened to become a full-time job. We were desperate to find ways we could help her feel better about herself. Kindness and reassurance were never enough to reach the lonely, empty place inside her. Soothing words fell on deaf ears.

We wanted Sally to get to know the horses. They would introduce something new and different in her life—an adventure—to help break up her repetitive behavior patterns. Sally had never been around horses and was terrified of them. We took her out to the corrals for her first contact. Madreperla, one of our mares and, coincidentally, also a "redhead," spotted the girl and made a direct and deliberate approach toward her, moving slowly enough so that Sally wasn't overwhelmed. She put out her hand and the horse sniffed it. Sally was proud of having the courage to extend herself in this threatening situation. She was also delighted by the velvety softness of Madreperla's nose. This small interchange was the beginning of a bond between girl and mare.

In the weeks that followed, Madreperla approached Sally as soon as she showed up at the corral. Gradually, the mare began to treat her as she would one of her fillies, calling to her in the same voice she would use to summon her own baby. Madreperla was clearly protective toward Sally and behaved as if she were somehow proud of her, gesturing toward us with her head the way mares characteristically do to show off a newborn.

An attachment between the two was forming. The mare was actively including Sally as part of her family group, and this was a brand-new experience for the girl. Incidentally, we knew Sally thought Madreperla quite beautiful and pointed out to her that both she and the horse were "chestnut" in color. Sally was delighted by this comparison. It made her feel even closer to the mare and helped somewhat to repair her self-image. The relationship she established with the mare became the solid foundation on which Sally's healing would occur. The last we heard, Sally had been adopted by foster parents and had gone on to high school.

Holding and Touch

Touch plays an important part in establishing the connection between horses and people. In infancy, the experience of feeling soothed is activated by our being gently touched and held. The positive impact this physical sensation has on us is retained in memory and serves to quiet our minds throughout life when we need comfort or to feel more centered.

The calmness engendered by touch nourishes us on many levels. We fortify ourselves with these tactile memories and experiences. Early in life especially, they foster development of an outgoing, adventurous attitude toward the world.

Through our tactile sense, we teach our whole being to be alert. Tenderness and gentility blossom from these simple experiences. Despite the severity of problems we face, just the memory of touch and comfort cradles our mind and allows it to be more open. When we call upon it we find ourselves effortlessly gaining inner peace, trust and vitality.

The healing influence of touch is illustrated in the case of Tom, a disturbed young 16-year-old in our residential treatment program. Tom had been becoming more phobic and was so paranoid he seldom left his house. On the few occasions he did venture out, he would never allow anyone to walk behind him. Tom couldn't attend normal school because once there, he would either lie on the floor or back up against a wall and refuse to cooperate. Up until this time, he had seemed a normal, very bright and extremely creative boy who excelled in his studies. As his behavior grew more bizarre, his peers started ostracizing him and he gained a reputation for being lazy and resistant.

We guessed that Tom suspected we intended to lock him away for being insane, but soon enough the boy began to see us for who we were and became confident that there would be no lock-up. As we treated him, it became obvious that his behavior was not due to a stubborn or antagonistic streak. He was, in fact, paralyzed with fear. We learned that he had only recently started refusing to leave his house because of a frightening incident he had experienced. He had been preparing to go out with his family one afternoon, and as he walked from his room to the front door, he was overcome by the feeling that his arms and legs were gone, as though they'd been amputated. The sensation could come upon him at any time, anywhere. Tom became convinced that someone "out there" was trying to maim him. Over weeks, these episodes came and went but became increasingly frequent.

Tom's parents took him for medical examinations. His physician, after conducting every medical workup imaginable, could find nothing organically wrong with him and concluded that the problems were emotionally based. That's when he was referred to us for treatment. We made no promises.

Tom had restricted his movements in order to protect himself from harm. There were odd nights when he would go out with friends, commit an occasional petty theft and stay out all night. After these forays, he confined himself to his room for days at a time. In his room at home, he remained in a fetal position, trying to embrace his entire body. At such times Tom felt he was, literally, holding himself together. In this way, he could gain a sense of physical wholeness. In a way, he was hoping for a rebirth.

After many months of treatment, Tom was showing good signs of recovery. He stopped isolating in his fetal posture, became more verbal and interacted more in his group meetings. We'd noticed that on those occasions when he felt able to go outdoors, he gravitated toward the animals. We asked if he was interested in trying something new involving the horses, and he eagerly agreed.

Tom was more receptive to the animals than to us, and we saw this as a way for him to see us in a different role. So often adolescent clients see therapists as rigid and unreal (which is sometimes the case). We're always looking for a means of breaking through these kinds of entrenched attitudes that keep kids in resistance. We found that the best way to turn this around is by being ourselves and getting involved, in the kids' presence, with something we truly enjoy and love.

Through this, we become real to them. For us, being with the horses serves this function well.

We got Tom started on a day when we were teaching some of our other residents bareback riding. He trusted it was a safe situation when he saw the horse was on a long line, so when his turn came, he willingly mounted the horse.

We couldn't believe that, for whatever reason, Tom felt enough excitement to get involved. We were so happy he showed any signs of life, so we moved quickly and without too much caution. If he didn't have time to think, he'd be less likely to become fearful. We hoped that Tom would focus his attention on the horse.

Atop the school horse, Tom wasn't frightened or distracted but involved and attentive. He seemed natural and comfortable and had surprisingly good balance and coordination. After a while, Tom asked if he could speed up to a trot. As the session progressed, we noticed that he looked relieved, as though his state of mind was anxiety-free and relaxed. When asked, he reported, "I feel like I am in one piece and safe. I can even feel my arms and legs. . . . I can also feel the strength of the horse."

In treatment, moments like this represent a crossroad. A door opens for us. Sometimes these events are subtle, but they're very important. Most of us miss them because we're looking for something grander and more profound. We were grateful for this brief moment—this small success—and knew we could build upon it.

Sitting astride a horse makes you powerfully aware of your own body as well as the one beneath you. Because the horse was, in a manner of speaking, holding him, Tom felt safe and protected—a welcome respite from his usual sense of extreme vulnerability. This, in turn, gave rise to a feeling of cohesion. Our first sense of safety outside the womb comes from being protectively embraced. We gain our original sense of self from our various physical sensations. This "body ego" lays the groundwork for the development of a psychological identity later on. This phenomenon of kinesthetic and tactile experience generating a sense of physical wholeness and well-being is a primary reason that mind-body activity can be so potent a factor in human growth. Tom's contact with the horse touched him physically and mentally, helping him regain the body identity he had lost when he had his first psychotic break.

Soothing experiences lead to an inner tranquillity characterized by alpha wave activity in the brain and are the precursors of hypnotic and meditative states that provide access to the unconscious. This access gives the client and therapist an opportunity to examine inner longings as well as deep-seated fears. Slowing down in this way and engaging in simple, sensual pleasures opens the way to discovering creative solutions to central issues.

Shifting the Psyche

The simple, direct approach to mental and spiritual health has been lost to us in our modern world. If we want to attain solace we need quiet time and to seek out activities that promote this. When we're in a worry-free state, even if only for a moment, the psyche can shift from a conditioned, analytical mode to a creative one that is conducive to profound change. These changes come from one moment of inspiration. It really doesn't take much.

The activities (or the inactivity of meditation) we pursue to slow us down must have a rhythm that is inherently healing. A rhythm that approximates the maternal heartbeat creates a sense of composure. The combination of rhythm and touch is a natural means of inducing a trancelike state. Conversely, arrhythmic activities are disquieting.

Hypnotist Milton Erickson describes this ordinary process as a period when an individual is open to change and learning is possible. Trance does not mean that a patient is put under or directed by the will of another. Trance, in fact, is a natural state that everyone experiences. It can be induced when we meditate, pray, or perform rhythmic exercises like walking or running. While in a trance, people have a clearer grasp of what their dreams represent. According to Sidney Rosen, "They are closer to what Milton Erickson called 'unconscious learnings' and less involved with thoughts and issues." [1]

In working with horses, which have a natural gait, attuning oneself to a specific rhythm is central to riding. The horse's rider or runner must learn to listen to make sure the horse is moving on a four-four beat with a point and counterpoint. The sounds of a locomotive or of castanets in flamenco music have a similar cadence.

The beat of a horse's smooth gait reduces stress. As the beat becomes more syncopated, a rider effortlessly relaxes into a natural alpha state. When patients who have experienced mostly internal emptiness or chaos sit astride a horse and begin to resonate with the mesmerizing rhythm of hoofbeats, their inner void is replaced by something like rapture.

In these sessions, we don't instruct clients to relax but rather, help them to find the proper rhythm and cadence.

Some clients find it helps to listen to music and follow its rhythm while they ride. This is equivalent to finding one's own mantra or focal point for meditation, except that in this instance, the horse and rider hold their mantra synchronously. Those who have had the experience of finding this rhythm, whether in the saddle or running beside a horse, report having had a sense of being rocked or cradled. We know that rhythmic movement facilitates growth in premature babies and that rocking chairs soothe fussy infants. All this early sensory input promotes growth and a sense of wholeness. It can do wonders for us no matter what our age.

The anthroposophist Karl König wrote that the horse's movement affects us in a way similar to a musical instrument. "Is not the horse's body comparable to a musical instrument on which movement plays its rhythms and melodies? . . . If any melody is to sound through this rhythmic locomotion, a man must mount the horse. As soon as this happens, gait and direction—under the rider's control—can become melodically effective. Now the frontal plane passes through the human being, joining rider and horse together; the two have become a unit. The horse gives the rhythm, the man the melody, and together they become a harmonious musical entity. This is one of the numerous secrets of the joy in riding: man and animal together become music—music that can be experienced." [2]

Participation in the Equine Experience, either through riding or simply watching the movement, sweeps us into the realm of feeling. It is equivalent to being absorbed in a symphony. We are enabled to circumvent our entrenched defenses and habitual reactivity. In this tension-free, passionate state, we lose our usual resistance and become far more receptive to new ideas and behaviors.

Several years ago we produced a national horse show to benefit the Shriners Hospitals for Crippled Children. We invited children who were physically able to attend. Most of these youngsters were severely disabled and recovering from catastrophic accidents. Some were burn victims. Most of them used metal braces or wheelchairs to get around. When they arrived, all of the children, many of whom had never been in such close proximity to horses, were very excited and quickly became engrossed in the show. They were captivated by the horses' beauty and as they watched them perform, managed for a time to forget their pain. Our hearts went out to these young-sters. We hoped to provide them with a little pleasure in the midst of their pain. To us, they were unsung heroes. We won-dered how often these quiet souls get passed by. It made us realize the importance of taking time to reach out and serve.

All the children present were delighted to be there—save one: a young boy who had sat along the sidelines, looking uninterested and angry throughout the entire event. One of the counselors took us aside to tell us that José was having a difficult time. He had been through a serious accident and subsequently undergone multiple bone grafts. His counselors were dismayed because since the accident, he had refused to participate at all in his own recovery. In order to heal himself, the child needed to work at walking—the only activity that stimulates bone growth. Instead, José wanted his caretakers to wheel him around. The counselors had tried—unsuccess-fully—everything they knew to motivate the boy but felt helpless in the face of his bitterness and despondency.

During an intermission between program events, we invited the children to come pet the horses in their barn stalls. All but José responded eagerly. We informed the kids that the horses had one request. They wanted every child who was able, to walk down to the barns. Those whose doctors said they needed their wheelchairs must come in their wheelchairs.

José's counselor never expected him to respond but approached him anyway to ask how he was going to get to the barn. To everyone's amazement, José asked for his crutches and walked. None of us expected this kind of participation from a boy who seemed so self-protective.

When he got to the stalls, we introduced José to the large chestnut mare, Margarita. We told him that because she was a Peruvian horse, she spoke Spanish (which was the language to which she responded). After that, we heard faint whispers as José began speaking to her in his mother tongue. As the mare came closer, we reassured José that she liked him and that there was no need to be afraid.

Sensing that José was mentally and physically fragile, Margarita touched his hand gently. José bowed his head and his eyes welled up with tears. Because he was very proud, he tried to hide his feelings, in spite of the fact that tears rolled down his cheeks. Margarita had managed to touch him in a way that his caretakers, regardless of their experience and good intentions, could not.

The children were gathered together for a group picture with the horses, and we brought Indomable and Margarita out of their stalls. The horses recognized immediately that these children were fragile and allowed themselves to be surrounded. The horses never shied or spooked from the children's unfamiliar metal chairs and braces, but stood quietly while the kids giggled and hugged them, calling out the horses' names. The resulting photo shows a smiling José. That image and that experience are indelibly imprinted in our hearts.

Other visitors to the ranch have similar experiences. While they're here, they become immersed in what's going on around them and manage to forget their difficulties—real or imagined. Whatever seemed so dire loses its charge as people effortlessly become present. Only the moment exists. This is an experience we hear repeatedly from our guests and clients.

The simple act of grooming horses is a powerful agent for promoting positive, regressive relaxation. It, too, involves tactile sense and rhythm. The mind slows down with each stroke of the brush or comb. Smoothing the horse's warm body, separating the mane to make it soft and silky, listening to the horse's breathing and witnessing its obvious comfort are satisfying. Breathing in unison with the horse induces a serene state, helping to further relax, expand and transcend stress and move toward an oceanic feeling of peace.

The Looking Glass

When we see our own behavior reflected back to us, we gain consciousness. A very astute professional woman who came to ride at the ranch shared an important insight with us. "Riding horses has made me so much more aware because they are so sensitive to my every move and feeling." In essence, horses give us living biofeedback because they show externally our inner processes. Sometimes what the horses reflect back is welcome and amusing. At other times, we wish we didn't need to look.

Horses detect involuntary physical reactions in us that result from our own unconscious fears and anxieties. Some people, when they're afraid, will collapse or fold and bend forward on their mount. An insecure rider may try to gain control by pulling nervously at the horse's bit. Others swing their legs. Each of us manifests our tensions in different ways that get magnified when we're astride a horse. When a rider is nervous or twitching uncomfortably, the horse visibly responds in kind. Likewise, a rider who is self-assured, confident and relaxed will have a confident, relaxed horse.

Once riders feel a horse's responses to their own movements, they can gain more control over themselves. In the words of one of our clients, "Atop the horse, the mind and body are working in concert—weaving, integrating—and the horse's appropriate response feels like the reinforcement. . . . I am holding the reins, clicking my mouth, keeping my feet back, standing up tall, imaging. We are not using spoken language, yet these things tell the horse volumes and we ride together. For me, this is exercising a kind of attention. If I drop the image from my mind, I lose focus. I lose a goal site and therefore, I lose the horse's energy. Ah, feedback!" Riders can also see how effective or ineffective their own style of behavior is. As soon as one modifies gestures, attitude and muscular tonus, the horse provides immediate feedback by mirroring the changes.

A riding student described an enlightening experience she had during a lesson this way: "I had been taking lessons for about 10 months when one day, I arrived in a foul mood following an unpleasant interaction with a client. The horse I rode, Margarita, was a gentle, patient teacher. She was very forgiving of my ignorance of riding and was doing her best to anticipate what I wanted when I had no idea how to send her clear signals. I had come a long way in my riding, and Margarita and I had started working together more as a unit. As I swung into the saddle and began the ritual walking that started every lesson, I thought I was leaving my dark mood behind me as I usually did when riding. But immediately I noticed a difference in Margarita. She wouldn't listen to me and fought me at every turn. There was an alien energy in her. She tossed herself willfully and alternated between an erratic trot that punished my teeth and spine and bursts of cantering that left my arms and shoulders sore from the effort of trying to rein her in. We battled back and forth, with me feeling increasingly frustrated and conspired against. I felt everything was out of my control and wanted to just sit in a corner and cry.

"Finally, I asked Deborah what was wrong with the horse. 'She's responding to your mood.' 'But she's never acted like this and I've come here in bad moods before,' I answered. 'Not anger,' replied Deborah. Suddenly, it became crystal clear to me what was going on. I hadn't even been aware that I was still angry, but Margarita had mirrored back to me perfectly what I was feeling. I saw my anger in snorting, prancing, willful display. Laughing at what I now realized was my own doing, my anger disappeared and I resolved to make it work between us. I concentrated on tuning both of us into a calmer place. She began to listen to me and we moved to a level of harmony we had never achieved before. I saw how my anger had been preventing me from having an effect on my world. Angry, I felt helpless and incapable.

"Margarita seemed to know that I could handle the lesson of seeing what I was doing, so instead of gentling me through the mood, she pushed me to the wall and made me take responsibility for it. Only when I took responsibility for my emotional state did I begin to have an effect. For me, this was a near-religious experience."

This mirroring occurs even when the person isn't atop the horse. The beauty of working with horses is that you learn time and again that you can't fool Mother Nature. Animals are reliable indicators of people's character structure because they so accurately tune into our psyches.

One of our exceptional adolescent cases provided us an important lesson in trusting our horses as well as our own instincts. We first met this boy when the probation department brought him out to the ranch for the equine program as an adjunct to its usual activities. Although Judson was on probation, he was the star of his county-run program and appeared to be a model kid. He followed the program rules to the letter and did well academically. On his residential unit at juvenile hall, when other boys fought, Judson would never be directly involved. Instead, he'd be watching innocently on the sidelines.

Our instant reaction at first meeting Judson was negative. In spite of all his counselors' reports of the boy's charm, congeniality and cooperation, we didn't trust him from the moment he set foot on the property. Our instincts were to keep an eye on him and make sure he wasn't up to something.

We felt like ogres for adopting an attitude that seemed so unfair. How could we be suspicious of a kid who, by all accounts, was trying hard to do well? We felt like two excessively judgmental paranoids. Nonetheless, both of us felt that something was amiss with this kid, and we couldn't shake that feeling, even when we tried. He was too flawless. Something about him was phony.

We were not alone in our personal assessment of the new arrival. Judson's phoniness became more obvious when he was around the horses. They intensely disliked something about the boy's very essence, and became highly agitated and bared their teeth whenever he came around. Mares near to him would swing their rear ends toward him in an effort to kick him or knock him down. The males would strike out at him with their front legs.

We recognized that, like us, the animals sensed something wrong, but at the time this was little consolation to our intellectual minds. We were still upset that we felt the way we did about the boy when there was no indication he was up to anything wrong. Our rational minds told us that our suspicions were unfounded, that he was, after all, only a boy, and that we should give him a chance. We continued to work with him.

For a time, Judson played at being involved and claimed he knew everything there was to know about horses. Over time, we noticed that he grew even less interested in the animals, possibly because working with them provided no rewards or privileges. When the other kids got involved with the horses, Judson subtly attempted to sabotage their work by making little quips that might be construed as just good-natured teasing.

Finally, the boy just stopped participating in the program altogether. He found that he didn't have the knowledge he claimed and was falling more and more behind the others in know-how and skill. Judson covered this up by feigning boredom. From this point on, he would lie on the ground and quietly act smug during lessons.

The facade Judson had constructed was sophisticated and quite convincing. He knew how to act appropriately in any situation. He was conciliatory when necessary, helpful and ingratiating when it served his interests. But watching him around the horses, it became more apparent to us that he was operating with a false self. If we couldn't trust our own instincts, we could certainly see the horses act on theirs.

Eventually, Judson was eligible for discharge from his treatment program. The staff on his residential unit had high hopes for the boy's success based on his exemplary behavior in the program. We, on the other hand, were skeptical. There was, however, no way to stop the wheels of justice, particularly on the basis of gut feelings. Because there was no good reason to prevent his discharge, Judson was free to return home. Just months after his release we learned that, while living at home, Judson murdered a four-year-old child.

Because of incidents like this, we have learned to fully trust the horses' responses to people. They rely freely on their instincts without second-guessing themselves. They were able to see past this boy's facade and recognize that he was dangerous, devious and evil. While the horses always seem to go right to the mark, our reasoning can get in our way, leading us to ignore important intuitive information. The horses' radar is uncontaminated by too much thinking and justifying. We humans would be better equipped to handle potential danger if we trusted our own instincts more.

We generally see "horse sense" displayed in more benign cases. In the course of a drug and alcohol rehabilitation program we ran, residents of another treatment facility were brought out to our ranch weekly, accompanied by their counselors. The group included a man, Randy, who inspired our distrust. Outwardly he was clean-cut, but he had a smooth manner that we found contrived and suspicious. He claimed that he was off whatever substance he'd been abusing. We were certain he was lying about it.

On one particular day, when the group arrived and began

walking around the barn, the horses began to behave strangely. The young horses panicked and the adult animals began to get agitated and unusually aggressive. We were heartened at the prospect that something real was about to happen for a change. We sensed that Randy was the source of their upset. His defenses were so slick that his treatment could have continued for years without his character being exposed otherwise.

Taking extreme care, we saddled the horses we regularly used for riding with this group. As Randy approached to mount, the normally trustworthy mare went into a hostile frenzy. She flattened her ears and bared her teeth—unmistakable expressions of mistrust and a clear warning not to approach. We asked Randy why he thought the horse might be responding to him this way. Her reaction was specific to him, so he couldn't deny what was happening. He was honest enough to admit he was under the influence of drugs.

The mare had exposed Randy, but because he liked the horses, he accepted the confrontation. Had we confronted him in the same way, he probably would have left the program. The mare made the job 10 times easier than it would have been otherwise.

Randy's counselors said they had suspected he was using but had been unable to prove it without drug testing, which was the next step they were prepared to take. The group was shocked to discover how violently the horse reacted to signs of substance abuse. Randy's usual defenses of denial and avoidance were useless to him under the circumstances. There is no way to argue with or discount the instincts of a horse.

A similar incident occurred with a client who returned to us many years after terminating therapy. Janet's treatment had helped her tremendously. Since we had last seen her, she'd earned an advanced degree in biochemistry, was successful in her chosen profession and enjoyed her work immensely. She had also managed to salvage an unstable marriage and raise two healthy sons.

In spite of the fact that Janet had attained a level of functioning she'd never known before, she still felt something was missing. Her only clear sense of this something was that it had to do with "communion." Her attempts to fill the void by delving into various spiritual practices had been unsuccessful. This is what brought her back to us. Janet was upset because spirituality "didn't work like magic." She had expected a miraculous transformation without having to bother with self-discovery.

Given her intellectual bent, Janet had long since analyzed herself thoroughly. She now spent a good deal of time and energy dissecting the psychological and motivational makeup of people who did not warm up to her. Janet found it unfathomable that people weren't drawn to her, and she took it quite personally. We liked her but also had difficulty warming up to her. We were at a loss as to what to do next.

Because traditional psychotherapy is structured in a way that we knew reinforced Janet's overdeveloped analytical side, we decided to have her work with the horses. Janet showed up for her first session eager and ready, but when we reached the stall her demeanor abruptly changed. She kept her distance from the horses and looked away with disgust any time one of them defecated or urinated. We couldn't believe what we were seeing. Never had we come across anyone who was so repulsed by such natural processes. She, however, was unaware that her reaction was unusual in any way.

Later in the day, with the prompting of another partici-pant, Janet petted one of the horses but recoiled instantly when the horse moved toward her touch. Her discomfort at this display of affection was so obvious that it surprised even her. The incident provided Janet with some insight into the fact that it was she who withdrew from closeness. She came to realize that she had always felt stiff around other people but never wanted to look at the fact that her own fear of intimacy was the source of that discomfort.

Janet's interaction with the horse gave her a graphic ex-ample of her distancing mechanisms at work and ultimately helped her dismantle some of the walls she'd so effectively constructed. Janet nicknamed herself "Ice Woman," but through her sessions with the horses she outgrew that title. She reported that the horses taught her not only to thaw out but to love. She began to relate differently to people, allow-ing more closeness and letting in warmth. Her need for com-munion was now getting fulfilled. We can all benefit from a glimpse into the looking glass.

If we had been working with Janet in a conventional office setting, she would never have had the chance to view that part of herself so graphically, and because she came across as much more open than she was, we could have missed the boat entirely. Even if we had recognized the extent to which she maintained her distance from others, she probably wouldn't have been able to see it for herself. The insight would have been nothing more than an intellectual exercise that we imposed upon her. People must be able to feel where they live in order to change themselves.

Compassion

Compassion is an important aspect of loving that evolves as a result of feeling loved. To have compassion means to deeply understand and feel tenderness for others based on who they are, as distinct from what they can do for us. It is a very sacred capacity and one that defines our humanity.

It is imperative that, as a species, we find our way back to the compassionate state that will guide us in balancing the "light" and "dark" elements of our character. Horses have helped us to evaluate an individual's capacity for compassion, serving as a barometer of the potential for change. These natural diagnosticians can size up a person's character within a matter of moments. The responses that animals have to people have to do with inner substance rather than outer facade, which is why horses can be so wonderful and yet seem so threatening to some people.

A person's reactions to the horse can be quite telling. Mental health professionals report that men and women who have perpetrated acts of extreme cruelty on others usually have an early history of animal abuse. As children, they are singularly lacking in compassion and perceive animals as objects. Later in life, this abuse extends to humans as well. The extent of the callousness exhibited by these people reflects the degree to which they are cut off from themselves. In the most extreme cases, we find that their loving, social aspects are undeveloped or altogether lacking, making it easy for them to objectify and dehumanize their victims. Their seeming inability to reverse roles renders them cold and distant and reflects how utterly cut off they are from themselves. Because they are so removed from their own feelings of vulnerability, through massive denial and avoidance, they are repulsed by acts of kindness.

Although this level of psychopathology is extreme, we have all, at some time or another, been guilty of merciless-ness. Our own evil is a fact we often choose to ignore. Evil is not just "out there" but is the shadow Carl Jung described as lurking within every human. Whether we like it or not, it is our legacy, part and parcel of the human package. To step out-side of our comfort zones and admit this takes courage, but without this sobering recognition we're more likely to lose our capacity for compassion, humility and forgiveness. If we lose our awareness of this side of our own nature, we risk becom-ing slaves to our own dark side. What goes unacknowledged in us has a tendency to grow larger.

Tenderness and compassion are qualities we must cultivate and never take for granted. This alone would make the world a better place by far. We find that, in order to further refine these aspects of our soul, it helps to spend part of our busy lives in the company of animals. It's an effective way to inoc-ulate ourselves against callousness. From animals, we learn about compassion and recapture our own generosity.

Our stallion, Trianero, has illustrated this poignant lesson to us time and again. One day he began crying in an eerie, high-pitched voice we had never heard before (nor since). We'd heard him vocalize in many different ways, but this call was anguished and constant as a siren. He ran back and forth frantically in his paddock, wailing continuously.

After assuring ourselves that Trianero wasn't in physical distress himself, we became convinced he was trying to direct our attention to some other crisis. We began searching the area for the source of the problem and were eventually drawn to whimpering and thrashing noises about a mile away from the stallion's paddock.

When we reached the spot, Trianero's cries finally stopped. A young filly was trapped underneath a fence, her legs twisted around and caught by the fence rails. She had obviously been there for quite some time. She was injured and exhausted, desperately trying to free herself. Her glazed, frightened eyes indicated she was in danger of dying of shock, and we were anxious to get her disentangled as quickly as possible. Although the horse suffered serious injuries, she eventually recovered fully.

The filly would likely have died had Trianero not intervened on her behalf. Somehow he had sensed the seriousness of her predicament and, since he couldn't reach her himself, made sure we took action. He had done everything in his power to get help. His compassion was heroic and touching.

This experience gave us some insight into this stallion's role as a protective sentinel. Trianero is not just breeding stock, but plays a much more critical part in his herd. Many times, we have walked with him and experienced a profound sense of serenity that's difficult to describe. Perhaps this is what it is to feel unselfish love. The horses' bonds with one another are not only touching but enviable in their depth. When we can learn to do the same for one another, our lives are bound to be richer.

5 The Genesis of Feelings

Man is an eternal pendulum of movement and vibration. His spirit is captured in a body in which forces throb and pulsate like the beat of a heart. Often they thunder and quake in his body with strong emotions that shake the very foundations of his physical being. Life goes on, rhythmically and quietly pulsating with the warm feeling of love or cascading with avalanches of violent emotion, for movement and pulsation is life. When movement diminishes, the person becomes ill, and when the movement stops, the person is dying.

—Dr. John Pierrakos, quoted in
The Secret Life of Plants

Feelings are derivatives of the survival instinct. Their job is to help us respond appropriately to our environment—to warn us away from potential danger and to move us toward what we need to live and procreate.

Without feelings, we stop being human, become cold and miss out on the richness of life. Without an understanding of them, we remain in darkness and confusion. When we attend to our feelings, they mature and blossom. Unheeded or denied a natural outlet, they impede our functioning and personal development. Our capacity to feel is an important part of our humanity and reveals our strengths and weaknesses.

Many authors have said that the heart is not just an organ but is the seat of our wisdom. In order to feel complete, we must recognize and accept the entire spectrum of our feelings and grow to understand them. Without consciousness of our heart's intelligence, we have but a limited view of the world. However, if we integrate and fine-tune this feeling realm of the heart, a door opens to mystical perception.

Because feelings are such potent indicators, we can use them to gain insight into the patterns of living and to karmic themes that we need to attend to and work on. One way to assess the depth and range of our own feelings is to monitor our reactions to situations, particularly novel ones. Do we love the journey and approach it openly, or are we just concerned with reaching the destination? Hence, we invite you, the reader, to become involved in a novel experience by getting to know horses in a different light.

The ability to be affected is important because it reflects a "response-ability" to life. The exposure of our psyches to healthy novelty is just the medicine we occasionally need. A slight shock breaks up the inertia and creates a flurry of feelings. This upheaval is a potential precursor to change; without it our psyches remain static, comfortably situated in the known. Individuals who continually play it safe in life, taking the path of least resistance and risk, deny themselves rich opportunities for personal growth.

Some people contend that they must conserve their outflow of feeling, believing that their inner resources are limited. The results of such misguided efforts are energy depletion and burnout. Most of us were never taught that movement and outflow free up energy. It's in our best interest to welcome novelty as an opportunity to build psychological and spiritual momentum. Movement is our greatest ally. However, it is also important to ask oneself, In what direction am I moving? Am I an individual who likes and feels more comfortable with inner movement or outer expression? Examining these styles gives us insight into where we need to work to reach our interior, the seat of mysticism and spirituality.

To venture inward toward our innermost sentiments opens our hearts: the fourth chakra in Hinduism and the area of heart-centered prayer in Christianity. When feelings are accessible and able to flow, we liberate ourselves from inner conflicts that inhibit our spiritual growth. It takes us out of our intellect. By discovering what resonates within us, we find a richness where our imagination becomes more vivid and can be launched into creative endeavors.

Personal expansion occurs by reaching feelings and leaving our defensive emotions behind. We human beings tend to overuse and misuse emotion; horses do not, unless poorly handled by owners. We frequently employ emotion and intellect as diversions to distance ourselves from what is churning inside. The difficulty in making this transition is that we often do not distinguish between the two realms. Differentiation requires nothing more than reeducating ourselves—learning to listen to our inner being, sitting still, being quiet and reflecting. In our intellectualized world we seldom pause to consider the force inside us, and yet it is one of our most vital resources. Without it, we remain stuck and fail to capitalize on all of our abilities. Cut off from our feelings, we experience an emptiness and yet do not know why.

One way to elicit and/or stimulate feelings is to watch horses. Imagine what they are feeling. Experience what sensations they bring up within you. See what happens to you in their presence. Temporarily shifting from a "doing" mode into a "being" mode can help us become more attuned and sensitive and to move from our head to our hearts. This teaches us to turn our attention inward and momentarily absorb ourselves in the feeling dimension.

Feelings and Emotions

The words "feelings" and "emotions" are two of the most frequently used and misused words in our psychological language. Although laypeople and mental health professionals use them interchangeably, the current usage tends to obscure the semantic differences between these words.

The verb "feel" comes from the Middle English *felen* and has to do with sensation and perception. A heightened feeling state is synonymous with passion, and a capacity to feel is the foundation for developing compassion. Feeling is also the perceiving of physical, psychological or spiritual energies.

"Emotion" is derived from the Middle French *emouvoir*, which connotes movement and behavior. Emotions are the outward expressions we use to either display or disguise an underlying feeling, matching or masking our inner state.

When expressed emotions are in accord with the underlying feelings, a sense of wholeness and harmony results—even though the feelings themselves may be negative, such as anger or sadness. Conversely, when emotions don't express the true inner state, this gives rise to a sense of division and disintegration. The distinction between these two modes of relating is important because the mode we use forms the basis of how we move through the world and how good we feel about ourselves in it.

It is impossible to exaggerate the role of the unconscious in the feeling realm. More often than not, people in the throes of strong feelings neither understand them for what they are nor know what to do with them. This is why clinicians advise clients not to make important decisions during times of crisis. Time is needed to sift through the layers of unconscious motivation and to develop awareness and clarity.

Feelings can be compared to clouds. They come and go and change constantly. Anyone who has been through a divorce or suffered a comparable loss knows what this is like. During the crisis, we may have a good explanation for what's happening and what we're feeling. Later, as our emotions (and our defenses) settle and we start to sort through the maelstrom of feeling, a whole new perspective emerges.

Emotions can be powerfully engaging, but they do not enlarge us spiritually. They are surface reactions that don't necessarily reflect the actual unconscious content. Since the "freedom of expression" movement of the 1960s, we have, as a culture, placed a premium on emotional expressiveness. It was during this period that the words "feeling" and "emotion" became so confounded, overused and abused. Encounter groups thrived on emoting—primal screaming, crying, angry confrontation, pillow pounding. The louder and more dramatic the display, the more authentic and profound it was assumed to be. Unfortunately, in many cases these groups simply made noise, while the deeper feelings of the group members went unaddressed. Participants left these encounters feeling as empty (though more stirred up) as when they had entered the group.

In therapy groups we led during the '60s and '70s, we were struck by the confusion about feelings versus emotions that was so pervasive among participants. We had organized separate groups to address different client needs. One group of individuals, identified as having psychopathic personalities, was sent to us by probation and parole departments in various counties. The other group, referred by hospitals and private practitioners, consisted of clients diagnosed as psychotic. Working simultaneously with these groups afforded us the opportunity to make some interesting comparisons of the emotional/feeling lives of their members. Examining on a continuum such personality traits as expressiveness provided a simple way to see how we are all, to a greater or lesser degree, very much alike.

These insights were a major impetus for us, opening our eyes and changing the direction of our work. We began to search for a new method to circumvent human emotion in a more expedient way and get to feelings, where real change is possible. We share this material with you because very few people ever have the opportunity to work day to day with the extremes of human behavior. It is these radical detours from the norm that often teach us the most about the multifaceted nature of our own human character. The knowledge we accumulated reshaped our thinking, moving our focus into the natural world to explore the idea of what happens to human beings when encountering a horse for the first time in the isolation of the wilderness, to take a hint from the Desert Fathers.

The Psychopathic Mode

Early on in our group work with psychopathic clients, the tears, screams, shouts and other antics we witnessed suggested to us that individuals in this group were feeling. With time, we learned that only our stomachs were churning. As therapists, we were feeling their "presented pain" for them.

We have all had the experience of being swept away by someone else's emotional state. During an especially engaging movie, it's easy to forget that the character we're watching is an actor playing a role. We begin to emote right along with the character. The psychopathic individual uses dramatics to manipulate and elicit the sympathy that he or she depends on for survival. Underneath, the person remains unchanged, using emotions not for expressing authentic feelings or artistic ideas but to con people. That's why con artists are referred to as "bad actors."

A woman in one of our groups fit this description perfectly. She had been incarcerated for mutilating her infant, and although she cried incessantly she could never understand why therapy was a condition for her parole. Another clue pointing to her lack of genuine feeling was that she cried for herself rather than her damaged child. Her tears flowed for effect, for the sake of her audience. She turned her tears on and off, depending on who was in the room. She would skillfully look to see how others in the group were reacting. When introducing her to horses in an informal way, she thought they were pretty but had no interest in them. She found watching them boring, and the horses showed no interest in her.

The psychopath's talent for "playing people like a violin" is neither feeling expression nor a form of intuition, but an uncanny ability to read people. Psychopaths can be frighteningly astute, picking up on defenses and vulnerabilities, attacking aggressively or seductively, praying upon others for self-satisfaction and a twisted form of pleasure.

In all human beings, there are many variations and degrees of this psychopathic tendency. For example, a milder rendition is a person who is self-centered and will do anything to get attention. Another is someone who always shifts the conversation back to himself or herself, disregarding the presence or needs of others, or an individual who only turns on the charm to get something in return, such as sexual favors, money, a free trip, or whatever is desired for aggrandizement or gratification. These are all milder versions of the same mode. All of us use emotions to get our own way from time to time, but the psychopath on the severe end of the scale uses them excessively. With "street smarts," the psychopath plays the game of time rather than living life authentically.

The psychopath's excessive and manipulative use of emotion protects him or her from perceived threats, both internal and external. For example, an internal threat might be a powerful and frightening feeling that finds outward expression through rage, tantrums, crying, screaming, pouting or all of these. The person may or may not be conscious of the underlying purpose of the display.

We learned through working intensively with psychopathic personalities that change can occur in some people, but because authentic feeling is lacking to some extent, change can be slow and tedious. In some clients, the resulting change lasts. In others, the change lasts only as long as an authority figure is present to keep tabs on their behavior. For this reason, working with this group can be taxing.

A necessary component of healing, if it is to occur, brings the very primary feelings of helplessness and emptiness into the person's awareness. Without this awareness, the psychopath's repertoire of feeling is severely limited. It is this pale inventory that seems to lead the person to take refuge in antisocial behavior. When working with psychopaths, therapists must be on their toes at all times, providing a sort of moving target so that clients can't quite figure out how to position themselves to manipulate or otherwise take control. As therapists manage to extract themselves from the clients' dramas, clients often begin to feel more vulnerable. At this point, therapy can really begin.

Retrospectively, if we had introduced this group to horses in a formalized way, their histrionic behavior wouldn't get them very far. Our horses relate to pure emotion as if it were noise. For example, when we first started our equine program, a man named Robert was sent to us for severe depression. He was very emotional, crying loudly, bemoaning his fate and whining about his failures. Robert put on a good show, acting very distraught. However, when trying to work with the horses he mainly attempted to dominate or manipulate them. He was constantly complaining that they "would not cooperate with him." As he walked through the barn, all the horses showed their teeth and tried to bite him as he walked by (and our horses do not bite). They showed absolutely no sympathy for him. He never noticed, but we did. Simply seeing the horses' reactions is a powerful evaluation tool. They conveyed more to us in a matter of minutes than we could have discovered by talking and probing. We have learned to read horses and their reactions toward humans.

That day, our perception changed quickly, and we had an evaluation in a matter of minutes. Through the horses' reactions, and by probing further, we discovered he was using drugs and had been conning doctors into giving him prescription drugs. We referred him to a drug and alcohol rehab program.

The Psychotic Mode

In contrast to psychopathic individuals, people suffering from psychoses experience deep feelings that they attempt to deny or numb by creating the alternative reality/fantasy system known as psychosis. While we may find comfort in distancing ourselves from individuals afflicted with psychoses and in seeing them as quite separate from who we are, it's useful to remember that we have all experienced psychosis, with its lack of defenses, as infants. In infancy we are in a state of helplessness. If it were not for our parents' nurturing and protection, we would not survive. Fears of annihilation during babyhood emerge for brief, transient periods. Our fears, however, are allayed as we are well cared for, and in time we learn to become more self-sufficient. In an individual suffering from a psychosis, these fears never go away, and their extreme dependency continues into adulthood. As adults, each of us exercises denial and engages in fantasy to some degree. It's necessary for our survival. The psychotic's denial and fantasy, however, are extreme, constant and disabling.

The psychotic feels without the defense of emotional tools, and inner terror is expressed in indirect and inappropriate ways. Psychotics can be very theatrical in trying to convey a feeling message. One group participant, a woman of Irish Catholic heritage, believed she was a Jew living through the torture of a concentration camp in Nazi Germany. Another, who believed his home was the sea, "became" a shark in order to protect himself. Another patient in the group experienced his feelings as an explosion. During a group discussion, he would suddenly begin to jerk and flail as he found his body parts dispersed in different areas as a result of a blast. Other patients assumed the roles of saints and martyrs, symbolically conveying their suffering and need for redemption/salvation.

Because psychotic individuals hide the intense feelings they experience, others perceive them as unfeeling and incapable of empathy. They have what is called "blunted affect," which simply means they show little, if any, emotion. They rarely cry, laugh or smile. When they do, it often doesn't fit the situation. They don't know how to use the customary guises and mannerisms we all rely on to get through a bad day. They can't put on a happy face. Although we may mask our feelings temporarily, once at home with loved ones, where it is appropriate, we can unload. However, psychotics can't do this. They rarely share their feelings with anyone due to lack of trust. When we first started to work with this group, we were amazed at how much the horses showed affection toward them and how they in turn loved the horses.

The rest of us find ourselves in the healthy range of the psychotic mode whenever we feel, be it positively or negatively. Stress or trauma that induces rushing sensations of despair, desperation, shame, guilt, sadness, emptiness, loneliness, helplessness or any other intense sentiment still places us in the healthy range. The only real difference between healthy and unhealthy people is that the former come to grips with their suffering, regain their equilibrium, and move forward with greater ease and awareness. For instance, after a death or substantial loss, we often feel raw and may withdraw, trying to weather the anguish and heartache. Seemingly unable to face another day, in time the healthy person finds ways to cope and bounce back. The people who are in severe psychotic states don't.

Nonetheless, when any of us is in a hypersensitive frame of mind, we too are capable of doing impulsive and self-destructive things. We have all heard tragic stories. A high-achieving businessman suddenly loses his job and can't support his family. In despair, consumed by feelings of failure, nothing else matters to him. Not wanting to burden his family, he impulsively commits suicide. A woman loses one of her children and goes into a state of depression for years on end, unable to resume her duties as wife and mother. Divorce is the solution she eventually chooses to remedy her situation, deciding consciously or unconsciously to wallow in her grief.

For people who normally function well, becoming overly sensitive is usually situational, brought on by such events as illness, divorce or job problems. Something happens in our lives that we cannot accept, control or understand. We never planned for it, so it throws us off kilter. For psychotics, every-thing is an unexpected event. As innumerable pressures mount, living feels like one big catastrophe. There are no intermittent respites from psychic pain. As children, their problems are often overlooked because of their quiet exteriors. Consequently, they seldom receive the help they need in the early phases of their disease. Their inability to express themselves continues until they break down and begin displaying bizarre behaviors. Their experience, given no functional outlet, leaves them vulnerable in the world. Without appropriate means of expression, they fail to develop a solid social persona to help them navigate through life.

Despite the intensity of their feelings, psychotics are unaware of the exact significance of their disturbed behavioral states. They often don't know they are behaving strangely. Their symptoms obscure the underlying sensations. Typical psychotic behavior—such as listening or talking to invisible people, withdrawal, speaking in coded and symbolic ways, blaming themselves for natural disasters or being frozen and mute—is not done so much for effect as to comfort themselves. Until they uncover the meaning of their behavior, psychotics experience a confusion and discomfort so profound that it moves them to exist, psychologically, in a parallel reality.

In the years following our initial observations, the horses have given us additional insight into this feeling/emotion theory. We have watched our horses and to whom they are drawn. Without question they prefer relating to people who are sensitive, even if their feelings are distorted. By contrast, people who are excessively emotional, without a developed feeling component to their personality, make them uncomfortable. Interestingly enough, our horses have been attracted to and curious about most individuals suffering from any kind of problem. They know something is wrong and will alter their normal behavior to make contact, approaching more slowly and carefully than the rest of us, knowing when they are kind but wounded. Time and time again we have watched our horses offer simple gestures of comfort and affection. Sensing an individual's vulnerability, they subdue their own exuberant spirit so as not to frighten them.

The two groups just described are out of balance; one tips the scale to the emotional end of the continuum and the other to the feeling end. Although these represent abnormal expressive modes, the abnormality is a matter of degree rather than form. At the ranch we strive for recognition and acceptance of the full range of our feelings, and for emotional expressiveness that reflects these accurately and still allows us to function fully in society. Using horses as a diagnostic tool to uncover defenses and symptoms, or to expose who we really are, has been very effective.

The Middle Ground

What can we learn from the previous examples? The most glaring lesson for us, working with both horses and people, has been the need to maintain a healthy balance between feelings and emotions. Horses, for example, will use both feelings and emotions to relate to one another. Much of what is communicated is nonverbal, via feeling channels, yet they also communicate by behaving in very theatrical ways, a flamboyance that usually directly expresses what they are feeling. They will become very showy when making a point. Exceptions occur when horses are mentally disturbed.

Like people, when subtlety doesn't work, horses will resort to something more effective. They like to handle small problems right away so that they do not turn into big ones, living by something like the rule of "give them an inch and they will take a mile." Overstepping boundaries, even if a minor infraction, creates uneasiness in the lead mare charged with herd safety.

We have two mares who are buddies. The lead mare in this dyad, Marquesa, is sensitive and very disciplined. The other mare, Malagueña, is sociable and fiery but often more child-like and rebellious. At mealtime Marquesa tells her friend to stay away from her alfalfa and eat from her own pile. When Malagueña listens there is little fanfare; when she doesn't Marquesa increases the emotional ante, first by pinning her ears back and motioning to Malagueña to get away by furiously shaking her head. If that doesn't work, she tries to kick. If her orders are still not obeyed, she resorts to a more dramatic display: Marquesa pins her ears back flat and chases Malagueña relentlessly at high speed. When her message has been respected and the boundaries reestablished, she stops. Once order is restored, they resume their friendship.

This resolution of conflict is not that different from what humans do when we have free access to both feelings and emotions. Yet horses don't analyze situations the way we humans tend to do. They just seem to know when it is natural to use feelings and when it is necessary to use emotions. Both play an important role in our lives. Learning to have the freedom to move from one realm to the other, depending on the situation confronting us, is invaluable. Sometimes we need to quiet ourselves and feel without any expression, while other situations call for drama.

Awareness of what we are doing and the ability to be spontaneous are key to maintaining this flexibility. We see an infinite variety of feeling/emotion responses in play regularly in our day-to-day lives. A father proud of his son or daughter will be outwardly exuberant, expressing his inner joy. A wife screaming at her husband, unable to get his attention any other way, appears angry, but this yelling is only a mask for her underlying feeling of frustration. None of these expressions are out of the ordinary. However, when our emotional expression is regularly detached from our true inner feelings, or we lose sight of the effect we are trying to achieve, we undermine our own direction and authenticity.

In comparing these styles, we have found horses feel most comfortable around people who have achieved a middle ground, have inroads to their feelings, and, when appropriate or necessary, outwardly express them in a real and sincere way. Domesticated horses living in captivity can trust them.

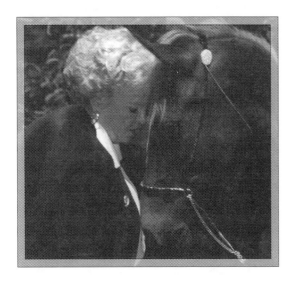

6

Instincts and Intuition

The human mind, freed from the
disturbances or "static" of restlessness,
is empowered to perform all the functions
of complicated radio mechanisms—
sending as well as receiving thoughts
and tuning out undesirable ones.

—Paramahansa Yogananda,
Autobiography of a Yogi

I ntuition is a direct perception of the truth, independent of any rational process. Even if you never plan on becoming an equestrian or owning your own horse, you'll find that interacting with horses is invaluable because they help you develop your intuition.

One can think of instincts as the hardware of intuition. Instincts are drives and behaviors that help guide us through a complex environment without having to stop and figure everything out. They organize our perceptions of what's going on around us in ways that are usually adaptive. Intuition, likewise, lets us see and respond to our environment without calling rational problem-solving into play. There is an organic knowing at work. In humans, instinct and intuition go hand in hand. If you trust your instincts, you probably have well-developed intuitive powers.

Instinct is a manifestation of divine intelligence that resides within all of us. By learning to listen to our instinctual hunches, we become more sensitized to the divine mind of the universe. Listening to our instinctive feelings is the forerunner to developing intuition. Instinct is nature's voice, our own inner receiver.

Activating dormant powers of intuition takes practice. If it is going to be available to us in our daily lives, we need to train and exercise it like any other latent talent. Horses provide a medium through which we can awaken and heighten our instincts. They give us an interactive and practical way to test our instincts and expand our intuitive communication capabilities, to monitor and fine-tune our intuition.

To work with horses most effectively, we must eventually get beyond technique and develop a sense of what to do. Riders test their hunches constantly and get instantaneous feedback as to whether their instincts are on target. For example, if a horse bolts, intuitive riders know—without thinking about it—why this happened and what to do about it. Beyond understanding essential techniques and concepts of horsemanship, they have developed confidence in their own sixth sense. Through experience it becomes second nature to them. Intellectual, technically oriented riders, by contrast, will often have delayed reactions or will overreact or intervene with horses in inappropriate ways. They are not in tune with their horses.

Some people get hurt around horses because they interact with them in superficial ways and remain detached, failing to recognize shifts in a horse's state of mind or body. By the time they intervene it's too late. Others concentrate more on the mechanics of riding, to the exclusion of other dimensions that are equally vital, such as heightening their senses or delving into the psychology or spiritual nature of the horse or themselves. This state of oblivion marks an insensate rider.

To ride with presence of mind, riders must constantly gather information from all over their bodies, from each of their senses, and finally, from their trained, well-exercised intuition. It also helps to begin to think like a horse, and over time, as you commune, "knowing" becomes more effortless.

Riders may find it useful to make up stories about what they imagine the horses to be feeling. Some people are so unaware of what's going on around them that they never consider the fact that the horse is communicating something to them at all times. They simply carry out the physical activity without any real engagement in what's happening. It never occurs to them that the physical and mental sensations they receive have any meaning.

A mare, Fantastica, stayed at our ranch until we could find the right people to buy her. She was from an unhappy home. She was a large, very sweet Peruvian mare but at times unpredictable under saddle. She had been hurt by someone in her past. When mounted, Fantastica was very wary of people. Periodically, for no apparent reason, she would shake and quiver, which was equivalent to panic attacks in people. If the rider noticed her inner state and offered a kind word or gesture, she would immediately calm down. Helping Fantastica required no physical strength or prowess, nor great equestrian skill. She generally was a very willing horse. Small doses of reassurance, such as saying "good girl," allayed her fears, and she would be trustworthy, responsive and cooperative. However, if the rider didn't recognize her feeling and intervene, she resorted to flight, taking off running. We were always present to help riders and intervene on their behalf. Nevertheless, it was amazing to us how many riders never felt a 1,000-pound horse trembling beneath them and her legs beginning to buckle. For those who did notice, their reflexes would be too slow and the problem would have already begun to accelerate by the time they reacted. We began to see how many different people have put their instincts on a shelf, even basic survival instincts. They lack the power of discernment and rushes of creative energy characteristic of a master equestrian. These riders must learn to observe and attend to a horse in a very basic way. Once they do, they can begin developing their instincts and awareness.

Awareness of self and others is the key. It means becoming intimate, having a friend where mutual respect is in action. Martin Buber developed his I-Thou theory because of a horse he came to love. The I-Thou theory helps us grasp the different styles humans use to relate in the world. When individuals develop a capacity to genuinely reach out and take interest in another, their style of relating is healthier and more interactive. They find that listening is the key, and they accept others' worlds and feelings without comment. Individuals move from a position of being self-centered and selfish into a more giving stance, where they are aware of the needs of others as well as their own. People learn to give as well as take, finding epiphanies in experiences with others, be they humans or other sentient beings. Reaching this I-Thou position is a precursor to divine communion or spiritual relatedness. Unfortunately, many of us lose sight of this basic requisite for good horsemanship or good partners in life. Overall, the formula for working with horses is simple and straightforward. If we want to maximize our successes, we need to build real relationships with them.

When a give-and-take relationship begins, riders possess a calm certainty and confidence, along with peace of mind. To achieve this, they must first still their bodies, then their minds, until they are quiet enough to exchange vital information with a horse. What's operating is a nonverbal understanding similar to that which exists between a mother and her infant.

Because the communication exchanged between horse and handler is often nonverbal, the handler/rider can't depend solely on verbal and intellectual skills. Instead, other ways of receiving and sending information must be found. When communication with the horse becomes more refined, the rider can use visual imagery and feelings to tell the horse what is wanted. To get the proper response, the rider must act in good faith. This means being free of inner conflict and, with all due respect, always asking the horse for complete cooperation. When the horse grants this cooperation, the channels of communication are open. This cannot be brought about by force of will or domination of one over the other. Nor can it be achieved by a passive rider who lacks discipline or guidelines for self or the horse. Horses do not trust or respect undisciplined handlers.

It often helps to ask riders what a horse is telling them as they work, or to ask them to reverse roles with the horse. Both of these activities serve to heighten sensitivity and increase our realistic perceptions of how our partner, the horse, sees us. Only when we stop deluding ourselves and look beyond can we begin to encounter mystery in the universe surrounding us. Keeping our own egos grounded by thinking of the horse helps. We learn in this way to develop other patterns of relating within the network of creation. For instance, we allow participants to experience, by way of role-playing, how they feel being nagged by a rider/handler or getting mixed messages, such as "Let's go faster, but if you do I will yank on you to stop."

Over the years, we have seen people relate to horses in a multitude of ways. One curious phenomenon is that many complete novice riders will ask, first thing, "Can I gallop my horse at high speeds today?" When we say no, most breathe a sigh of relief. For many, the closest they have ever been to a horse is at the movies or on television, and so they have some preconceived notions. Others want to go out on the trail before they have any experience or knowledge. It is obviously false courage because typically those who are the most impulsive can barely keep their balance in the saddle. Riding for them at this stage of the game is pure fantasy. They never realize that until they can recognize and define their own parameters, they will confuse the horse.

By contrast, riders who are more experienced or other-oriented often have a healthy respect for the animal. Preferring not to take foolish chances, they wisely get acquainted before going on a joy ride. Savoring the developing intimacy is what matters most to them. They also often lack the unnecessary embarrassment new riders feel when recognizing their own limitations. Free from childish fantasy and images, they use their imaginative powers differently, increasing their ability to intuit. Consequently, horses feel more secure under their direction.

In working with horses, we must examine our ingrained belief that humans are preeminent in the scheme of creation. By doing so, we can learn to overcome the superiority complex plaguing the human species and place ourselves in an equal position with our fellow creatures. Horses generally respond better to people who are at ease with themselves and have nothing to prove.

When riders experience blocks, we may ask them to assume the role of a mare or sire (mother or father) to the horse. This exercise calls for role expansion, from human to horse, and role transcendence, shifting from male to female perspectives and vice versa. New insights emerge when riders walk in different shoes, shaking their tendency to habituate.

If a problem arises, we may also instruct the rider through guided imagery. For example, if a rider is constricted by too much technique, we may suggest imagining it is the first time on a horse. This introduces a sense of novelty to the situation and helps the rider let go of preconceived ideas, embellish on this fantasy and enact the fantasy in the saddle to see where it goes.

Problem-solving is one of the best ways to become inventive. Facing an immediate dilemma stretches our minds and teaches us to reach into other dimensions. An example of this occurred with a beautiful chocolate-colored filly named Alicia. We not only saved her, but we now own her. The previous owners had been neglectful and abusive. It was obvious she was psychotic. At a year old she was in constant terror, trying to defend herself in any way possible. Malnourished, she was skin and bones. No one could put a hand on her easily because she was so scared. The day we went to pick her up, she ran in tight circles in her small dark stall. No light came through, adding to her sensory deprivation. The manure was up to her knees.

At the sight of people, Alicia rushed toward them showing her teeth or started to climb the walls, a warning to keep away from her. The former owners admitted they didn't know what to do with her. They said she had jumped a five-foot fence when they put her outside in a corral. She had not been out of that black box or handled in six months. By the grace of God and our team of workers, we got her in the trailer and took her back to our ranch. Somehow she was able to maintain minimal composure on the ride home, seemingly aware we were getting her out of a hellhole. She held on to her sanity by a thread. However, it was short-lived; once situated, her habitual terror returned. The entire story of Alicia is very moving but lengthy, so we will save it for another time. The point is that we were faced with a big problem: handling a filly who was "mad."

We put her in a space smaller than one of our large corrals so we could begin to catch and handle her. Our stalls are 30 feet long, open and light, and the horses can see one another. We had the job of sitting in her stall and calming her.

Sitting with an emotionally disturbed horse takes tremendous faith and patience. There are no recipes and no books that substitute for hard-core experience. It is just you and the horse. Each horse is different. It helps to experience or think of horses as individuals with individual personalities.

We went in day after day for about six weeks. One of the most productive things to do is nothing. Just being there with true sincerity and love is half the battle. When you emit kindness, horses begins to experience you as a benign presence. Once horses become curious, you are on the road to success. When this happens, they edge toward you and retreat. They will look at you for a few seconds, then quickly turn away, shifting their eyes to and from you. You must sit quietly and let it happen. If you intercede too abruptly, you interrupt the process and sometimes have to start over again. You must learn not to interfere in the unfolding process. Nonetheless, in getting to that workable place, you sometimes begin to wonder if anything is going to work. Doubts run through your mind, like "What if they never change?" Thoughts cross your mind, like "What if I can never get a halter on this horse?"

In working with very emotionally disturbed people, you might think, "What if they never utter a word again?" The content may be different but the feelings are all the same. Learning to contain and control our human anxieties is a key ingredient for a successful outcome. Once we calm ourselves, we make room in our heads and hearts for new ideas. One must expect a positive outcome with people and with horses, no matter what it takes.

As we sat in Alicia's stall on a daily basis, our minds began to wander and we suddenly remembered something we had not thought of in years. In training and raising big cats, a past hobby, we would whisper to them. Once, in a moment of desperation with an unruly female cat, we got an impression. It may sound strange, but when you live with animals long enough and become intimate, you begin to get impressions from them. Through impressions animals convey what you need to do, or what they are trying to communicate. Native Americans can hear the stars talking when they are really patient and at peace with themselves. Receiving mental messages or pictures is only another facet of our intuition that we have allowed to go dormant. Under the right circumstances, it can return again.

When we whispered to our female cat, the cat happily rolled over and forgot her anger. After trying this technique and feeling encouraged, we had another idea: to start communicating with cats in more creative ways by following their feline rituals and customs and imitating their mannerisms. They would purr and we would purr back. We developed an ability to make cat sounds that were uncanny and very close to the real thing. Soon our cats began to relate to us differently by being more attentive. They seemed to respect us as "mother cats" because our behavior was disciplined and soothing.

Horse Whispering

Whispering to animals, horses in particular, is not just a matter of softening your voice. Whispering, in our experience, is
more than a physical act: it is a state of mind. It is whispering
with your heart, like another horse softly nickering to its young.
It is born from a pregnant silence, requiring a deepening of the
handler's feelings, going inside the self to a place where love is
pervasive. In this state we momentarily suspend many of our
normal human concerns and constructs. To be successful, one
must be totally unruffled by external concerns and feel an overall sense of peace and stability. One cannot feel rushed or pres-
sured by expectations. There must be no sense of urgency,
thereby overriding the dimensions of time and space, no fear of
appearing foolish. In this climate the whisperer develops a keen
ability to see beyond convention and reshape reality in inge-
nious ways, even when faced with the impossible.

We believe the act of whispering works because it also creates a sonic vibration with a resonance that is captivating to
the ear and, like poetic verse, alluring to the inner soul. The
content or message of the whisper must be conveyed by way
of feelings, drawing upon the sacred language also prevalent
in verse. We found when we verbalized a truth to the horse,
instead of a shallow or superficial utterance, we got a better
response. We have theorized that saying something pointed
gathers energetic intensity and becomes meaningful to the
horse. Although the creature may not understand the words
we use, we have found it understands the handler's intentions
and mental impressions. To make contact with another creature at this level affords us the opportunity to feel a special
union, but whatever you whisper must be meaningful.

When we tried whispering to Alicia, she came closer. It not only worked, but it began to speed up the process. Alicia made a huge about-face. Not only did she change, but she has become one of the most affectionate, gregarious and trusting horses we have. It was after this 180-degree turn that we began to probe further, searching the literature for anything we could find on communicating with horses. We discovered a wealth of material in the Celt/Iberian horse literature. In the process, we found out about a man named Dan Sullivan, a 19th-century horse tamer from Ireland, known as the original "Horse Whisperer." Henry Blake, an English horse trainer today, uses many imitative techniques to calm the problem horses with which he works. Blake wrote about "horse whisperer" Dan Sullivan many years ago.

Somehow people from diverse cultures and backgrounds on separate continents are all tuning into each other by way of a common link: the horse. Through watching this phenomenon, we have learned that if any of us submerge ourselves in a discipline—be it art, music, philosophy, psychology, math, horses, dogs, et cetera—and love the subject matter, eventually others will also stumble upon the same methods and ideas. Vital knowledge is transmitted without ever reading or talking to each other. Knowledge, in essence, does not belong exclusively to any one individual, but to the universe at large. Men and women who are open simply receive it nonlocally, by intuitively tapping into these specific "fields." Seeing this phenomenon in action is a real tribute to the work of Dr. Rupert Sheldrake, the acclaimed biologist, who recognized this process and developed his theory of morphic resonance. As Dr. Sheldrake maintains, "If we are influenced by morphic resonance from a particular individual to whom we are in some way linked or connected, then it is conceivable that we might pick up images, thoughts, impressions, or feelings from them, either during waking life or while dreaming, in a way that would go beyond the means of communication recognized by contemporary science. Such resonant connections would be possible even if the people involved were thousands of miles apart. Is there any evidence that such a process actually happens? Perhaps there is: for such a process may be similar to, if not identical with, the mysterious phenomenon of telepathy." [1]

Equestrian tact—knowing whether and how to apply aids with a horse—is also a good index of a rider's intuition. The rider must stay relaxed and open. Emotional upheaval in the form of preoccupation, worry or obsession interferes with intuitive processes. A quiet mind and body open energy channels and lead to healthy, self-induced trance states or altered states of consciousness.

Intuition develops more strongly when the rider and horse have a feeling rapport than when they are distant. Sensitivity to one another is heightened by the presence of a feeling connection. The diminished gap promotes a sense of unity and a meeting of the minds.

Horses teach us to expand our consciousness by going beyond the human realm. They connect us with divine mind. Working with horses makes this experience tangible. To be in tune with a horse is to be in divine attunement, or at one with nature.

Horses trigger healthy excitement and alertness. The rider must stay awake on the horse, calling all senses into play. Intuition is dampened when participants are bored. Boredom makes us dull-witted, and then we operate below our potential. Piquing curiosity and interest removes blocks and mental sluggishness, helping us become poised and ready to receive and be touched by "Great Spirit," as our creator is called in Native American traditions, or "Holy Spirit" in Christianity.

In order to use our instinctual gifts and innate talents productively and responsibly, we need to practice shifting between reality and inner imagination, rationality and irrationality, thought and feeling, science and magic. In our day-to-day lives, many of us operate primarily in one mode, exclusive of the other.

We know of many extremely creative individuals who are so unanchored in the practical world that they have difficulty taking care of their basic needs. These people haven't cultivated basic survival instincts or a stable foundation for themselves and are severely impaired as a consequence. Such a person essentially behaves as an empty vessel that becomes charged with flashes of inspiration and creative energy, only to be left empty once the flashes subside.

An excessively practical person, on the other hand, has well-honed basic survival instincts but little else to put toward personal development, and is unable to transcend the exigencies of daily life in order to enter a realm of finer, spiritual instincts. Such individuals are cut off from God within.

For balance in life, we need to practice something that grounds us in the practical world yet leaves room for mystery and fancy. This shifting between and blending of our two natures can help make us whole.

The Grounding Nature of Horses

Being around horses and seeing what instincts they are endowed with have a stabilizing effect on humans and fill us with a great sense of wonder. Having this opportunity has been a great privilege for us. Often we come away with more questions than answers. This is how life is supposed to be. Sometimes we are meant not to know but to wonder and let the mystery unfold.

The following two stories demonstrate the bittersweet. They are situations about which we can only imagine what really happened. In fact, we do not know, but we believe that in our compulsive society, suspense can be a welcome reprieve. Leaving situations unresolved and finding a balance in paradox can be stimulating to human growth and intuition.

Last year a friend phoned in distress. His four-year-old Peruvian gelding was out of control. Fred, a high-powered businessman, traveled extensively and was away for long periods of time. He always tried to hire the best people to manage his ranch but discovered it didn't always work. He learned that while he was away, one of his ranch managers had singled out this horse and beaten him. When Fred found out, he fired this man. Nonetheless, the damage to the horse's psyche had already been done. The gelding wouldn't let anyone near him. When people came too close he used his front legs to strike. His eyes rolled around wildly, trying to see everything at once. The other workers on the ranch wrote the horse off as crazy. The horse was suffering not only from trauma but also from being ignored by the workers assigned to his care. Fred loved this gelding and was desperate to see if he could remedy the situation, so he brought him to us.

When we first heard about the horse over the telephone, we wondered if it was sensible to take him. Maybe he was too far gone or had grown to hate people too much. However, we could empathize with Fred, so we reserved judgment. When the horse arrived, we got some very strong first impressions.

Walking off the trailer, the horse's eyes flashed, his mind elsewhere. What frightened people the most was that he looked so menacing and crazed with his ears pinned back, threatening to strike or kick and then unexpectedly lunging forward, charging toward people. He could not even walk in a straight line.

It was obvious that the horse's immediate concern was survival. He was not mean-spirited, only defending himself from an overpowering sense of vulnerability and fear. He was fighting for his life. In spite of this stance, we could feel tenderness, a very lovable quality. Standing near him, deep feelings of sadness and loneliness arose in us. Sorrow surrounded him like a giant cloud. His heart was broken. We recognized the pattern because we had felt the same thing in the presence of many of our psychotic clients, who behaved violently. This horse had become so disconnected from the world around him, he did not even know or answer to his name. We put him into a stall, talked to him and did nothing more.

We did, however, ask Fred if we could change his horse's name, giving him a Spanish name instead of the English one he had. Our friend agreed. We came up with the name Santiago Saint James. Saint James is the patron saint of Spain, and the Cathedral of Santiago de Compostela in northern Spain was erected in his honor. It is a sacred site, and throughout history a thriving center for pilgrims. During the Middle Ages it attracted thousands of pilgrims seeking healing, miracles, solace, rejuvenation, spirituality or a respite. It is also a popular holy and mystical place for modern-day pilgrimages. Saint James is revered for his dedication to Jesus, having been one of his prominent apostles.

His symbol is the cockle shell. As legend has it, James was also known to come out of the sea riding a white horse covered with shells. We figured Fred's horse needed the guidance of a saint, and so did we.

Much to our surprise, within 24 hours he had calmed down. We attributed this miraculous change to the horse grapevine, which is a way horses communicate with one another on a ranch as soon as a new horse arrives. In some way they fill the newcomer in on what it is like, how the owners of the ranch are, whom to get close to and whom to stay away from. It is no different from when we get a new job or attend school: there is usually someone there to lend a helping hand and show us the ropes. If the resident horses are relaxed and comfortable, the newcomers will usually adopt the same demeanor and attitude. If the horses are nervous and agitated, the new horses will be wary and anxious, if not overtly hostile. It is very important to know the tone of your herd because they have a strong and profound influence on other horses that come into the group, particularly those that are already insecure. They can make a human's job very easy or very difficult. This is basic group dynamics. Nevertheless, we knew that Santiago's ongoing training would be tricky, bringing up issues of trust. We started his education from scratch, as if he were a foal, and we began to repair his shattered sense of confidence in humankind.

In a very short time he worked his way into our hearts. During his respites from terror we could see a gentleness in his eyes. He exuded a kindness. Seeing glimpses of the real Santiago, we knew when the time had come to trust him and present him with more challenges. We knew when he was ready to be ridden for the first time. Although his behavior had vastly improved, we knew that his potential for becoming dangerous was a reality. Longstanding terror is not easy to overcome. We were also aware we were newcomers in his life.

After being saddled, Santiago walked apprehensively through the corridor on the way into the riding arena, passing our oldest stallion, 23-year-old Trianero. Santiago was anxious, naturally fearing the new and unknown. As Trianero went by, Santiago stopped dead in his tracks. We had a distinct feeling Santiago was not resisting, only listening. Trianero had something to say to him. The two of them stared at each other in a way none of us had ever seen before. There was obviously some kind of communication going on. It was as if Trianero sensed Santiago's distress and was reaching out to comfort him while protecting us, seemingly cognizant that of all the horses on the ranch, Santiago could be a time bomb and needed extra support. Nobody moved. This silent exchange went on for about three minutes. When it was over, Santiago was more relaxed and confident.

Santiago entered the arena like a different horse. Mounting, which could have been traumatic, was not. There was no bucking, wheeling, rearing or kicking. He acted as if he knew what to expect, and yet this was the first time he had ever been ridden. The biggest issue for him was a fear of falling, a common occurrence in horses first undergoing saddle training. However, in Santiago's case this was very pronounced, creating a real and ever-present potential for panic. Feeling the initial weight of the rider, he did not want to move. He grasped the ground for dear life, almost hugging the earth. We sensed he was more worried for our safety than his own. Yet we did ride him that day. We often wonder, what did Trianero really say?

How all of this happened so naturally and smoothly is still a mystery, but we have our theories. We could look to the obvious and say it was the all-encompassing environment of love, discipline and understanding. However, we firmly believe that it was Trianero's loving intercession.

The next story happened to a horse from another ranch and was told to us by the owner. It is about an exceptionally loving, level-headed and gentle mare, Alegre. Due to her incredibly kind and self-sacrificing nature, she had become a horse anyone could ride, particularly children. One spring day a group of kids, part of a youth group, and their parents went on a trail ride. Most of the kids knew about horses, but one young girl was a complete novice. She was assigned to Alegre. The trail they took had always been well marked and an easy one to travel. However, due to winter rains the group ran into some unexpected terrain. They could follow only a narrow path on the side of a hill because the rest of the road had fallen away. It was impossible to turn back. The kids were instructed to get off and walk. The young girl was scared, threw her body weight to one side, and the mare went off balance. Alegre began falling off the side of a cliff with the youngster on her back. Both adults and kids saw what was happening and were horrified, but there was nothing anyone could do.

What happened in just a few minutes seemed like an eternity. Trying to help in some frenzied way, one man looked into the face of this mare and said the scene will haunt him forever. He saw terror in Alegre's eyes, not for herself but for the child on her back facing death. There were no words, but he could read her. He saw her struggling, using her hooves like claws to hold onto the side of the mountain, as if she had grown talons. He also said that the way she continued to hold onto the side of the cliff was physically impossible, but she would not let go. He could hear the mare communicating with the girl, as if she were screaming "jump off, get off now, jump." Alegre was still holding on for dear life, while the earth beneath her was crumbling. She yelled "jump" again. Finally, the panic-stricken youngster got enough courage and jumped to safety. As soon as the girl reached the ground, Alegre let go, fell into the canyon below and tumbled to her death. The people witnessing this tragedy said they were convinced the mare made a conscious decision to save the girl. However, we will never really know. Their belief is based upon hunches and feelings and therefore impossible to prove.

What we can conclude from these stories is that the basic nature of horses is loving and expansive. They have even been known to create new situations to ensure no one in the herd is isolated and lonely. For instance, some males form bachelor herds in the wild for companionship if there are not enough mares to go around. Fellowship is vital to their mental as well as physical existence. Without an active community, they become depressed.

We have always known horses love one another, but until we lived with them, we never realized how deeply they love us too.

Being Oneself

Learning how to be oneself comfortably is among the most challenging tasks in life. To accomplish it, we must live life, not analyze it. This is a simple concept that is difficult to enact. In the beginning of our careers, we spent countless hours constructing a professional identity, only to discover that to be truly effective, we had to dismantle that professional persona and relearn how to be natural, how to live close to our God-given instincts. Instincts are our guide for behaving in a way that is appropriate for our species.

Instincts and intuition are inseparably linked. They are the tools we're given to maneuver our way through the world. Each animal, each person, is endowed with the resources needed to have direct access to God's wisdom, if so desired. If cultivated and used properly, instinct and intuition can become the God within. If they are ignored, the individual simply exists or, worse, is destructive and careless.

Many recent books on spirituality discuss the concepts of "divine mind" and "interconnectedness." We made these constructs more real by journeying into the world of animal energy and instincts. We learned that the instinct within each of us is a reflection of the larger universe.

When we appreciate our own inborn resources, we begin to discover some of nature's mysteries and rhythms. In comprehending these forces within ourselves, we can unlock an endless reservoir of energy. Our instincts become our personal connection to nature—a way of reminding ourselves that we are part of the indivisible whole.

For the most part, our Western culture has put its efforts into developing intellectual, technical and material prowess. We use these assets to hide, manipulate and distance ourselves from others, and ultimately, to gain power and control. Our powers of the mind are no longer used just to gather and process information from the world around us, but have evolved into one of our greatest weapons against ourselves and others. Connecting with the mind of the horse, whose instincts are intact, lets us regain our own sanity and peace of mind. Observing the instinctual powers of the horse at work reminds us we are capable of reclaiming ourselves, if we can revive our dormant instincts and awaken our intuition.

7 Taming the Instincts

When man is in a healthy state, his life is a constant creative process. He is inundated by feelings of love, of oneness with other human beings. . . . In the diseased state, the first characteristic is that reality is distorted—the reality of the body, the reality of the emotions and the reality of the true nature of other people and their actions. Evil, then, is a distortion of facts that in themselves are natural. Because the sick person does not perceive his own distortions, he feels that the ills in his life and his functioning come from the outside. . . . His thinking is limited. His feelings are expressed by hate and brutality and cruelty, fear and terror.

—John C. Pierrakos, M.D., "Anatomy of Evil"
in *Meeting the Shadow*

Horses teach us how to tame instincts and show us graphically what happens to us if we don't —how we are capable of acting toward one another if our instincts go astray. For this reason, a discussion of infantile instincts in human beings can help us comprehend and prevent many of the social problems plaguing us today, such as violence and hate. It is important to remember that peace begins at home, inside our own skins. Placing the locus of control where it belongs is empowering. Awareness of this responsibility gives each of us, in our own small way, the opportunity to participate in making our homes, schools, workplaces and streets better places to live, to stop perpetuating the same vicious cycle by passing the buck or looking for grandiose social or political schemes to solve our own unrest.

When we begin to explore these dynamics in the light of day, it helps us adopt a new and fresh perspective about human interaction in general. Understanding another's point of view, even if we disagree or disapprove, teaches us compassion, the key ingredient in conflict resolution. By developing the ability to momentarily suspend judgment and unravel some of the psychological and spiritual barriers confronting us, we are more apt to find constructive solutions.

Building bridges, however, is no easy task. Trying to find commonalities instead of differences takes a willingness to remain open, without prejudice. Despite our idealism, human beings, if not made conscious and aware, are prone to regression when introduced to conflict or stress. All of us, despite our level of education, sophistication, economic class or social standing, are capable of behaving in immature and childish ways. Sometimes this is healthy, but much of the time it simply undermines our potency, such as when we jump to conclusions, quickly condemn or become emotionally inflamed.

However, once we grasp the various nuances of exchange that can transpire between people in our day-to-day lives, we have an opportunity to interact in more effective ways, particularly those situations in life most fraught with animosity and conflict that cause us stress, upset and a general feeling of dis-ease. Delving into the world of untamed primitive instinct teaches us how to avoid seeking refuge in our own infantile impulses and how to relate on a higher plane called civility, where we maintain our composure even when we are being pushed or tested to act otherwise.

Horses like to test our fuses because it tells them what kinds of human beings they are dealing with. For instance, our mare Maria was a rebel who liked to distract her various riders by not going in a straight line. Even though she knew how to go straight, she would make zigzags, almost daring riders to react negatively. The riders who got angry at her made her accelerate. Instead of ceasing this annoying behavior, Maria would continue it and become more provocative. By comparison, the riders who tried to regain their own composure, refrain from blaming anyone, take a deep breath and start over, trying to figure out what they could do differently, charmed her. After passing the test, she performed beautifully.

In *Meeting the Shadow*, Dr. John C. Pierrakos described disease as a state in which the individual's energy and consciousness are not unified or balanced. During these episodes of disorder we can backslide to an earlier stage of development in the human life cycle, such as infancy or childhood, when our instincts were untamed, self-serving and very primitive.

When the dark aspects of character are overrepresented, we harbor greed, envy, jealousy, rage, lust, domination, bitterness and hate, which results in mental strain both for the individual in question and the recipient of the exchange. To experience any of these feelings to some extent is human, but when someone is consumed by them and gives them excessive time and attention, the experience becomes distorted, the person becomes possessed, the emotional fire is fueled and the individual becomes destructive. This sort of imbalance is widespread in our present cultural climate.

Comparing raw human impulses and tendencies with those that have undergone a process of taming, by way of education and refinement, is useful. Comparing our human methods of socializing with Mother Nature's, via observing horses, also helps us gain insight.

Infants—human beings without independent locomotion —are submerged in a psychological world. Although physically helpless, as infants our imaginations are active, producing dreamlike images and hallucinatory experiences and softening the reality that we are entirely dependent on the outside world. Infants are also exploding with unrestrained energy and impulses. At this phase of development, we humans are at our most bestial, and our unconscious is a cauldron of excitation. This is a natural state of being. Unable to crawl or walk, we pose no threat to others. But later in life, if we don't outgrow these processes and tame our instincts and impulses, we may resort to impulse-ridden, psychotic or socially inappropriate behaviors. If mitigated by the outside world or indulged, these primitive instincts grow in strength and consume the personality. It is the same difference between a wild horse and a domesticated one.

As we become socialized, our instincts lose their wild character and are redirected into channels appropriate for our society. There is much speculation as to why some people outgrow their infantile, impulsive natures while others retain it, and on many levels, how socialization actually occurs remains a mystery.

Horses, for example, are socialized into the herd by their mothers through strict discipline and nurture. Stallions will also partake in child-rearing, disciplining foals if they are close by. Neither mare nor stallion, with few exceptions, tolerates antisocial behavior or attitudes in its young. Horse mothers, as we have said before, are tough. They are non-permissive as a general rule and expect their young to abide by the rules. It is also common knowledge that the mares who discipline their foals make it easier for humans to educate their offspring. By examining the behavior of mares, humans can learn how to better educate their own offspring. Mares who are strict teach their foals to learn subtle forms of communications, think better, have longer attention spans, control themselves and not overreact. These are all useful skills that make it easier for the horse to focus during training with human beings. Very few mares are indecisive or anxious mothers. When they are, the rest of the herd gets angry.

We care about your opinions. Please take a moment to fill out this Reader Survey card and mail it back to us.
As a special **"thank you"** we'll send you exciting news about interesting books and a valuable **Gift Certificate.**

Please PRINT using ALL CAPS

Name
First _____ MI. __ Last Name _____

Address _____

City _____ ST __ Zip __

Phone # (__) __ - __ Fax # (__) __ - __

Email _____

(1) Gender:
___ Female   ___ Male

(2) Age:
___ 12 or under   ___ 40-59
___ 13-19   ___ 60+
___ 20-39

(3) Marital Status
___ Married
___ Single
___ Divorced/Widowed

(4) Did you receive this book as a gift?
___ Yes   ___ No

(5) How many Health Communications books have you bought or read?
___ 1   ___ 2-4   ___ 5+

(6) How did you find out about this book?
Please fill in ONE.
1) ___ Recommendation
2) ___ Store Display
3) ___ Bestseller List
4) ___ Online
5) ___ Advertisement
6) ___ Catalog/Mailing
7) ___ Interview/Review (TV, Radio, Print)

(7) Where do you usually buy books?
Please fill in your top TWO choices.
1) ___ Bookstore
2) ___ Religious Bookstore
3) ___ Online
4) ___ Book Club/Mail Order
5) ___ Price Club (Costco, Sam's Club, etc.)
6) ___ Retail Store (Target, Wal-Mart, etc.)

(9) What subjects do you enjoy reading about most? Rank only *FIVE*. Use 1 for your favorite, 2 for *second favorite, etc.*

	1	2	3	4	5
1) Parenting/Family	○	○	○	○	○
2) Relationships	○	○	○	○	○
3) Recovery/Addictions	○	○	○	○	○
4) Health/Nutrition	○	○	○	○	○
5) Christianity	○	○	○	○	○
6) Spirituality/Inspiration	○	○	○	○	○
7) Business Self-Help	○	○	○	○	○
8) Teen Issues	○	○	○	○	○
9) Sports	○	○	○	○	○

(14) What attracts you most to a book?
(Please rank 1-4 in order of preference.)

	1	2	3	4
1) Title	○	○	○	○
2) Cover Design	○	○	○	○
3) Author	○	○	○	○
4) Content	○	○	○	○

TAPE IN MIDDLE; DO NOT STAPLE

**NO POSTAGE
NECESSARY
IF MAILED
IN THE
UNITED STATES**

BUSINESS REPLY MAIL
FIRST-CLASS MAIL PERMIT NO 45 DEERFIELD BEACH, FL

POSTAGE WILL BE PAID BY ADDRESSEE

HEALTH COMMUNICATIONS, INC.
3201 SW 15TH STREET
DEERFIELD BEACH FL 33442-9875

FOLD HERE

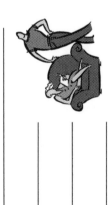

Comments:

Musica, a mare staying at our ranch from another breeding farm, was very immature in her temperament even though she was five years old. When she had her first filly, she was very apprehensive. Her foal ran wild and she was constantly running after her. The foal became more and more hyperactive because the mare waited too long before reprimanding her. Usually foals are taught to stay by their mother's side immediately after birth, unless given permission to do otherwise. This mother and foal were constantly disrupting the peace and well-being of the rest of the group. This went on for several weeks, until one day the other mares, deciding to take matters into their own hands, bit the childish mare for being passive. Then one of the older and wiser mares took the foal under her wing and disciplined her. Within one day, this out-of-control filly had manners and respect. Musica was also ostracized by the other mares, who chased her around the paddock as if to say, "Now how do you like it?" The inert mare learned from the herd pressure to take responsibility, which saved her next foal from the same fate. What does this say about our recent "anything goes" or "let the little darlings express themselves" attitude toward child-rearing?

Horses also like to strike while the iron is hot, while humans, with their intellectual defenses and endless excuses, often minimize the problem at hand. Hoping to avoid conflict and have the problem disappear by magic, people often wait until it's too late. Time and again in our therapeutic work with people, we have seen small problems mushroom into real human tragedies. More often than not, casualties could have been avoided if it had not been for someone's "well-intentioned" avoidance and procrastination.

In the horse herd, love and discipline are inseparable. You

cannot have one without the other. Unfortunately this is not true of all humans, some of whom believe they can love their young without teaching right from wrong. Love can be a powerful incentive for individual growth, appropriate social functioning, and repairing broken or strained relationships. However, without first neutralizing raw instinct through discipline, we are incapable of using the love we have been given toward a productive end.

We see many humans incapable of loving due to un-neutralized instincts, humans whose aggressiveness is not used toward a constructive goal but is instead self- or other-destructive, humans whose capacity to love diminishes and in some cases extinguishes itself. Fighting, aggression, jealousy and competition do occur between horses. However, with some exceptions, they usually take place with preservation and protection of the individual and the herd as their aim. Male fights are more goal-oriented and specific, such as a stallion guarding his mares, or for territory. The mares rarely fight with any intensity, but when they do they can be very brutal to one another. Typically, this type of fighting between females happens when two dominant mares are vying for a leadership position and one of them will not give up.

We have always wondered why some very young children are responsive to love, affection, and affirmation and have no problem grasping the principle of give-and-take, while others have greater difficulty with it and, in extreme cases, are completely unreceptive to it. Some of these children are in a constant state of agitation, and nothing seems to comfort or quiet them. Although we can't answer this puzzle, we do know that it's critical to help these individuals, at any age, become more receptive to love. Without this receptivity, the individual's impulsiveness will rage on, controlling his or her life. He or she may not be able to accept what is good in the environment, but will instead develop an attraction and proclivity for what is negative. When this happens, the individual fails to become a team player and likes to incite trouble instead. The provocateur derives power from making others uneasy or igniting their fuse. What is challenging is how to most effectively interact with and manage this type of individual, who is becoming more and more prevalent in every facet of society and is taking control, undermining forward progress in others, and disrupting the health and harmony of others.

In taming instinctual behaviors, we can begin a sensitizing and civilizing process to make others more aware of and open to the presence of love in the world. Without this, there is little hope that they can grow up as functional adults capable of experiencing the full spectrum of human feeling.

Fear and Aggression

Love is the synthesizer responsible for helping us integrate the multiple facets of the soul—our core being. It gives us the courage and strength we need to be creative. In spite of our willingness to give love and the obvious benefits of receiving it, some individuals are simply not prepared to accept it. If the individual is full of rage and/or terror, love's positive effects are usually obliterated before they can be influential. Introducing love prematurely, in the form of kindness and gentleness, can sometimes do more harm than good. Some people display a toxic reaction to it. Loving kindness makes them feel cornered, and they respond with escalated violence, hostility and fear. Nonetheless, love and affection must be constantly maintained in the background of any vital environment. When the individual is ready to receive it, it must be available.

We have learned this very lesson from horses whose owners have failed to handle them on a regular basis. For example, a deprived horse who is not used to being touched or groomed will jump or leap when brushed. Even though the handler is well intentioned, doing something very positive and comforting by our standards, the horse doesn't interpret it that way. Therefore, until the horse gets used to the sensory or tactile input, the handler must move deliberately and slowly. Lacking a former reference point and unaccustomed to human touch, the neglected horse experiences "care" as something endangering it. People who have had little emotional input are the same way.

A realistic appraisal of an individual's frame of reference helps us know how to approach. Meeting people on their instinctual turf, rather than on our own, makes the interaction more palatable to them and fosters openness.

Horses teach us how to zero in on each others' instinctual development and become, as a result, more flexible in our social interactions, more able to approach and retreat mentally and physically when appropriate. When we can understand others, we are less apt to take things personally and get hurt or offended. It aids us in the art of conflict resolution and helps us develop the skills necessary to channel our own energy into finding imaginative solutions. Horses also teach us not to fear the new and to break free from what is habitual and familiar.

What typically keeps us from change is reverting to old familiar behaviors, even if they are counterproductive or painful. Carl Jung described the deep and superstitious fear of novelty expressed in people from certain cultures. In Jung's words, "The primitives manifest all the reactions of the wild animal against untoward events. But 'civilized' man reacts to new ideas in much the same way, erecting psychological barriers to protect himself from the shock of facing something new." [1] For some, the expression or display of love or kindness is a foreign experience to which they may or may not be able to adapt with time.

Anger blocks creativity, as our instinctual energy is used to prepare for "the fight." Chronic anger depletes our creative reserves. In and of itself, anger is not a feeling but an emotion that masks underlying fear or hurt. It can be likened to our physiological response to stressors. For instance, in a threatening situation the adrenal glands secrete hormones that allow us to engage in "flight or fight." Likewise, anger is an instinctual defensive posture that, at least temporarily, gives us some semblance of courage and power to handle a situation we perceive as dangerous. In dealing with chronically angry individuals we all come into contact with, be it at work, school, church, social functions, et cetera, we must learn to curb our own anger if we expect them to soften. We must help others rechannel the protective, instinctual fears that keep them resistant to and distant from others.

Horses have taught us about the transfiguring effect of reducing anger. We have repeatedly observed that they rarely show offense at a handler who reprimands them legitimately for something they have done wrong, if the handler is devoid of rage or vengeance. However, if reprimanded in a fury, horses will counterattack because they feel challenged. Many power struggles can be avoided by learning not to meet anger with anger. This is an invaluable lesson in life. Developing patience and being unemotional is the key. In psychotherapy we call it professional detachment—which is not the same as being uninvolved. On the contrary, involvement is an important expression of interest and a necessary ingredient to good relatedness, be it with humans or horses.

Michael came to us for lessons on his own stallion and was angry all the time. On his horse, he was so distracted by his own anger and bitterness that he couldn't think of anything else. He was absolutely uninvolved with the immediate task at hand. Some days Michael was angry at his boss or coworkers. Other days he was angry at his kids or wife. He would take this out on the horse, calling him stupid and yelling obscenities. Each time he rode in this state, the stallion would try to knock him off by rearing and lunging toward a wall or fence. Michael was even angry at us because we wouldn't give him any quick tricks or techniques to fix the situation. However, we did have others ride his stallion so he could "see." With others his stallion was always well-behaved and very cooperative. The stallion was so willing, we had his six-year-old son ride him one day. Not only did the stallion love and take care of this child, but he also obeyed him. When Michael saw this, he wasn't pleased. His first reaction was rage and jealousy. However, by the next lesson he had had enough time to think and simmer down. He returned much less defensive. Once he learned to control his own anger and become more tolerant, his stallion automatically quieted down. He didn't have to do anything to the stallion once he changed his own attitude.

If we hope to resolve conflict we have seen repeatedly, it is best not to counter in anger. Ferocity, when it is used by people or horses, is a way to warn others not to come too close. By respecting boundaries and remaining cool, we can usually defuse hostility. Fighting back to prove a point, which many are inclined to do, only accelerates the problem. Adopting a nonreactive approach to hostile behavior often piques the interest and curiosity of people accustomed to provoking others with their anger. Teenagers are masters at trying to get their parents to blow up; when a parent succumbs, the child gets the upper hand. Fighting with a horse, particularly one in a state of agitation, evokes an equivalent dynamic. Most people who have any common sense won't try because nobody wins. The wise individual learns to transcend the situation, rising above pettiness and primitivism, not wasting time in the mire, and looking instead for creative and novel ways to make inroads. Skilled horse trainers and therapists alike are expert at using their active imaginations to find fresh solutions, not getting themselves sidetracked or entangled in a web of instinctual defenses or habitual regimes.

To establish an initial connection and dialogue, we must meet people at their present level and not force progress or force them into our mold, which is soothing in itself. Being truly with someone, rather than attempting to manipulate them into another position, leaves no opportunity for a fight and has a powerfully calming effect. In most cases, when given the freedom to be who and how one is, an individual will spontaneously open up and become more cooperative. Often, the rage drops away and we can at last approach on a new level.

Being nonreactive to destructive or hostile behavior does not imply passive acceptance of it. Rather, it means we need to deal with it, take off our blinders and see the unacceptable. To redirect the destructive energy, we must dance with the shadow, not kill it. When we can achieve this stance, we learn to confront maladaptive or nonproductive behavior matter-of-factly, without becoming embroiled in the heat of our own emotions. This nonreflexive style of being in the world is potent.

Troubleshooters are more effective when they are able to detach themselves from their own emotions and become dispassionate about results. By not pushing a rigid mental agenda, or a need to retaliate or control, negotiations usually can have successful outcomes. By suspending judgment, trying to be fair and remaining open-minded, we learn to strike a fine balance between confrontation and true understanding. Learning not to condemn or jump to conclusions opens the door to new courses of action and ideas. This quiet inner attitude is fertile ground for endless opportunities and teaches us how to meet difficult challenges in spontaneous ways. Only in this neutral posture can we overcome the obstacles we meet in some very difficult situations, with some very trying people. Working with gang youth is a vivid case in point.

Working with Gang Youth

Prolonged anger is perhaps the most ruinous state an individual can maintain. It is a wasted expenditure of energy. Sustained anger and hate should be considered red flags, signaling deep human pathology. It tells us the person's destructive urges are running rampant. Until these urges are contained, nothing gets resolved and the person remains dangerously unpredictable.

Beware of people who can't subdue their hate. The malevolent energy wields tremendous power over people, and they will become slaves to their own impulses. Once they cross the line and revel in the stimulation that anger stirs up, they become even more susceptible to its influence. Raw, primitive feelings begin to erupt indiscriminately and involuntarily, and they start to behave impulsively. This is the cycle we hope to stop.

While consulting with various probation departments, we have worked with and observed this behavior in teenage gang members—a tough and challenging population. Although these adolescents include males and females, we're addressing males here because they're far better represented in the groups with whom we've worked.

Gangs are characterized by a strong pack mentality. Their members typically come to us in a posture of flagrant disrespect. These kids view adult rules as suspect, discipline as cruel and social skills as irrelevant. They do not respond particularly well to a soothing, caring approach. In fact, they loathe and are made wary by people they perceive as too nice. If you understand instincts, this maladaptive response becomes more comprehensible. A caring attitude is useless with gang members because they have an overdeveloped pack mentality that is fueled largely by aggressive impulses. At this level of personal and social development, one cannot reason with them.

Traditional forms of therapy aren't effective for gang members with a history of committing serious crimes. If the treatment they're given doesn't capture their wholehearted attention, it will fail. Making an impact on these kids (some are young adults), who are very detached, is difficult. Many have stopped caring about much of anything, including life. From a feeling standpoint, they are, in a sense, anesthetized. If any change is to occur, they must come to their senses and reattach to life.

To help these youths become more receptive to intervention and treatment, we get them working with horses. The object is to break through the wall of anger and aggression with which they surround themselves. The novel experience of handling a horse elicits a mixture of excitement and apprehension in these kids—when one of them begins to really develop a relationship with a horse, he finds that he can't apply his street smarts in this new environment.

The most defiant adolescents are aware of the potential physical peril involved in being around animals this large and powerful. They realize they cannot fake it around the horses. If they want a safe interaction, they must learn the rules, traditions, formalities and finesse of horsemanship.

From the beginning, then, two important components are set into place. First, the teen is effectively removed from a comfortable context in which his aberrant behavior works in his favor. Second, he finds himself in a highly structured situation in which his well-being depends upon his paying close attention and observing a set of rules. This sets the stage for effecting change.

We treat the teen's relationship with the horse as living theater, wherein sooner or later, his personal internal dynamics unfold. The feelings that the horses often inspire of being off-balance and in imminent danger are powerful catalysts, as long as they aren't excessive or too long-lived.

The vulnerability that this novel situation evokes in people is natural. Originally, the stage-specific helplessness marking infancy and early childhood forces us to turn to our parents for protection and guidance. If it weren't for this sense of vulnerability, we would never form attachments to others. In normal children, the need for protection fosters the perception that parents are powerful, caring and important beings. The parents' physical size also inspires the child's respect and humility. This healthy phase of dependency and parent worship instills feelings of elation and admiration in children for their parents, but it also evokes feelings of trepidation. During this phase, the parent/god is omnipotent—all-loving and wrathful.

Horses inspire a similar mix of emotions. In adolescents (and adults), horses naturally evoke feelings not experienced in years, if ever. In gang youth, this emotional storm reverses the dominance roles. The delinquent boy instinctively recognizes that he now has an adversary he is unequipped to overthrow or control.

Once we break through the immediate barrier of hostility, we introduce the adolescent to different experiences. Novel, healthy diversions have a positive impact at this point and help diminish the energetic intensity of instinctual impulses. Through a series of playful exercises, we demonstrate the horse's amazing sensitivity and responsiveness to subtle physical and mental communication. These teens are invariably shocked when they realize that the horse is much more likely to behave well with someone who is open and vulnerable than with someone who is aggressive and pretending to be courageous.

We teach the boys what the Spanish word *macho* means by introducing them to a stallion. We explain the role of the stallion, its behavior and breeding within the context of its social group. Then they learn about the mares' role as leaders and strong, maternal protectors. Finally, when we introduce them to the four-month-old foals, the boys learn why discipline is so important. Through watching a mare discipline her foal, they see that discipline is basically an educational process to which every young mammal is subjected.

As part of the program structure, we use the horses to teach the kids discipline. They become responsible for grooming, mucking the stalls and feeding the animals. Once they've mastered these skills, it's time they learned how to ride. Lessons in basic equitation (riding on horseback) follow. For the first month or so of instruction, the gang youth look at us as though we're speaking a foreign tongue. Yet soon the giggling, the sly exchange of glances and the eye-rolling stop, and most of the kids give the horses and instructor their undivided attention. Even some of the toughest gang members can hardly wait until it's their turn to ride.

Having thus transformed themselves into true students, they learn the fundamentals and classical art of horsemanship. They begin to comprehend the principles underlying all the classical arts—form, balance, roundness, harmony and lightness. One might assume that gang kids would automatically reject this kind of instruction. However, once their defenses have been effectively disarmed during the initial lessons, they embrace it eagerly. They become enamored with the information and enthusiastically take it all in. These teachings appear to fill an emptiness in these boys. Art is, after all, food for the soul. These youngsters have largely been deprived of it.

We're often asked why we don't teach these kids something "practical." The fact is that what we teach is highly practical. It's important to understand that riding is not just a physical exercise but a mental one as well. The kids learn they progress not by using brute force but by engaging in a team effort based on respect, sensitivity, trust, caring, focused attention and, of course, discipline. They learn a level of fine body control that is far beyond what they're accustomed to practicing.

Equitation requires that the rider sit tall and proud. One needs to develop an elegant carriage to elicit the same from the horse. Acquiring mind/body discipline and skill in working with horses elevates riding to an art form, and riders must learn this connection. The horse will respond to what the rider visualizes. If an adolescent can conduct himself this way within the program setting, he will carry these new skills with him into the larger world. What could be more practical?

The style of riding instruction we practice incorporates the dramatic elements of mystique, myth, adventure, intrigue, fantasy, history, dance and music. It awakens the students' dormant imaginations. When they are infused this way with healthy excitement, buried hopes and dreams begin to emerge. Creativity is awakened in them through working with an animal they have come to respect and admire. Through the medium of the horse, their reality is enriched and they acquire a new perspective on life. Here the violence ends.

In working with delinquent youth or teens in general, much of the instruction we devise gives them some very unique educational and creative opportunities. These lessons have been so helpful in stretching their imaginations that we now adapt some of these techniques to adults as well. We set the stage by giving historical information that is fraught with adventure. By introducing the notion of the quest, individuals or groups find the activity of riding or working with horses even more captivating.

Our Peruvian horses are naturals, since their own backgrounds are so rich and intriguing. Not only do we have the mystery surrounding Peru to draw from, but we also have their ancient lineage, which dates back 25,000 to 30,000 years (B.C.). Cave paintings found in the Valley of the Yehwahs

(Valley of the Mares) in Malaga, Spain, show horses wearing an early rendition of rope halters and being led by man. For centuries Iberian horses have had an illustrious history on the Iberian peninsula and throughout Europe, and eventually became the horse of conquerors as well. What better grist for conjuring imagery full of myth and love?

In the beginning, most of the delinquent youth we worked with were so surly and belligerent that no one, including us, could have imagined such a turnaround. However, once we managed to guide them in tempering their instinctual impulsiveness, they became quiet internally as well as externally. Eventually they expressed tenderness and a longing to get close.

After participating in the program for a while, most of the teens we work with begin to soften and actually adopt a more childlike demeanor. Curiosity, enthusiasm, eagerness, and even helpfulness and cooperation begin to appear. This is what happened with Frank, a 17-year-old Latino gang member and juvenile hall parolee who had been in and out of serious trouble multiple times. When he first entered the equine program he adamantly refused to participate, preferring instead to sit on the sidelines showing his complete lack of interest.

Asked if he liked horses, Frank responded with a sharp "no." Pushing him into participating would have simply fueled his dislike and distrust of adults. With kids that are sizing us and the program up, it's better to stay out of their business altogether and let each participant come to his or her own conclusion about each of us.

In keeping our distance and respecting their need for room, we make it possible for them to lose some of their resistance to us and to the situation. Under these circumstances, if they do respond, it is their choice and not ours. This gives them a healthy sense of control in decision-making.

In the beginning, Frank clearly held us in contempt. As far as he was concerned, all adults were phony—particularly ones who were ingratiating. We never pressed the issue and let him be. Frank held on to this attitude for a month or so.

While we were instructing one of the kids on the proper way to place a Peruvian saddle and bridle on a horse—a 500-year-old tradition and rite of passage in Peru—Frank was, as usual, sitting on the sidelines and seemed oblivious to what was going on in the arena. The girl we were working with just couldn't remember what to do, although she was trying very hard. Just as she was ready to give up, Frank jumped in to help her.

In spite of his studied appearance of indifference, Frank had not only been listening and watching through weeks of instruction, he had committed what he'd heard to memory. He gently guided the girl through each step of putting on the tack in the traditional way. We commended Frank on his knowledge and on his willingness to help. Later, he admitted to us that he'd harbored fantasies of helping others but had found no meaningful avenue for doing this in his community. He had brought his leadership abilities into a neighborhood gang instead.

During his initial weeks of sullen silence, Frank had listened intently to the stories of ancient Peruvian and Mexican civilizations, to the history of equitation, and to tales of the great horsemen. He wanted to learn more. Because he was of Central American heritage, Frank was especially interested in stories of Mexico and its indigenous people. We spoke to him at length about Mexico's rich culture, the pride and creativity of Mexican musicians, dancers and other artists. We talked of the people's passion for bulls and horses, their deep faith in God, and the enormous emphasis on family life.

While all this information intrigued Frank, it also seemed to make him sad. He had always dreamed of going to Mexico. We told him that the Peace Corps had opportunities for helping people throughout the world, including Mexico. An excited Frank asked if we thought he himself could ever hope to be a Peace Corps nurse or medic. This was well within his reach, but we told him that in order to do it he'd have to continue through school. To our surprise, Frank stayed with this line of conversation, even though he had always believed schooling to be totally irrelevant to his own life.

Soon thereafter Frank came to tell us he wanted his tattoos removed. He shared with us his surprise that we'd never mentioned them in the first place. Now he wanted us to speak to his counselors at juvenile probation about helping him get the tattoos off. Frank's tattoos were removed with laser surgery.

Following these events, Frank participated fully in the equine program. He also became genuinely involved in outside classwork and began to formally learn Spanish. Frank, now "Francisco," had found the seeds of his identity and a vision for his own future. Two years later he was off to the Peace Corps.

Sexuality and Delinquents

Understanding sexuality is an important part of human life. The sexuality of horses is a natural example of passion and intimacy. Learning to understand the horse at this level can give us insight into some of the complexities of this human desire as well.

Our raw sexual drive directed toward each other is referred to as animal attraction. We have all experienced it, especially as teenagers. It is unadulterated lust, which some people confuse with love. The individual, overcome with biological urges, craves discharge. If you want to understand this raw urge, observe the sexually excited horse, who displays it very graphically.

Yet it is amazing that a stallion with seemingly limitless passion can learn to master and channel it. He knows that a mare must give her consent. Brute force and raw sexuality do not impress her. The stallion woos her by being patient, loving and tender. He learns to win her affection by transforming his raw desire into an expression that is pleasing to her. He often accomplishes this by putting on a magnificent show.

The way the stallion transforms himself during his dance of passion is called "natural collection." He gathers the energy of his excited state and uses it to sculpt his own body into a living work of art, arching his gloriously crested neck and swelling his whole body beneath it, like dancers collect themselves in preparation for the dance. The ability of the horse to become an arc instead of a linear form enables him to execute harmonized movements of the most beautiful kind. With leaps and pirouettes often performed in slow motion, he looks as if he is flying and dancing on air. This transformation renders absurd the claim of some human beings that they cannot control their impulses. Like the horse, we must develop our sexual repertoire from the crude to the spiritual if we care ever to experience the sublime. Without the seeds of tenderness and love, we can never hope to elevate our sexual energy into a passion for life or *agape*.

Watching this expression is impressive to anyone. The

delinquent boys, trying to impress everyone with "war stories" of their own sexual escapades, stop in the presence of horses, most particularly stallions. The real stallion in a state of arousal is awesome, and boys almost always settle down and drop their obscene talk in the presence of such equine behavior.

One group of delinquent boys from juvenile hall came to the ranch with their probation officers in spring when we wanted to breed one of our mares to a young stallion. This breeding would be a first for this inexperienced stallion. In his exuberance he failed to take time, lacking awareness and sensitivity to the mare. Instead of making love talk and listening to her cues, he became consumed by his own excitement and rushed on top of her. Even though the mare was in full heat, she was so angry at him she kicked him and he fell off her. The breeding was unsuccessful. We asked the boys who were watching this travesty, "What do you think happened?" When they didn't come up with any answers, we added, "Never give a boy a man's job."

Curiously, mature stallions behave differently around teenage boys. Sometimes the stallions become provocative by parading and strutting, almost as if daring the boys. When the boys show their respect for their position and authority, the horses accept them. In this way stallions father upstart colts.

8 Disciplined Play

I was by his side, a master craftsman,
delighting him day after day, ever
at play in his presence, at play
everywhere in his world, delighting
to be with the sons of men.

—*The Jerusalem Bible,*
Proverbs 8:30-8:31

The capacity to play at any stage of life maximizes our ability to learn new things. Play helps us work through problem areas in our lives that we may otherwise avoid because they are too painful. It enlivens our journey and teaches us to transform states of personal disorder into creative order. Play infuses self-discovery with lightness, and it lends an element of excitement and adventure—even pleasure—to what can be a painful, serious path.

Whether the play is mental, physical or both, its most important feature is that it reaches us at a deep, subliminal level. It activates the imagination, where all things are possible. Through playful imagining, we begin to discover innovative ways to practice what we need to learn or create in life.

Many people think that acting silly or being raucous is a form of play. Although this may help us feel better at times by providing some sort of comic relief, it often falls short of teaching us valuable lessons. The play we are referring to is more complex. The play activity we engage in must help us reach hidden dimensions of the soul. To do so it should have a structure, format and order. With these, the play form is more apt to provide us with a corrective emotional experience.

Structure simply makes exploration safe and gives it direction. The activity should never become dull or regimented.

Organizing our world gives us a foundation to fall back on. Rigidly systematizing our actions is something altogether different. Without spontaneity and surprise, our lives begin to resemble the lives of institutionalized people—a monotonous existence that takes a serious toll on the spirit. In "The Psychiatrist and Chronic Mental Illness," Hilary Sandall describes the effects of any treatment that becomes a humdrum routine. "Hospitals, nursing homes and boarding institutions with house rules that regiment the lives of their residents produce dependency, apathy, lack of motivation and other characteristics of the most chronic forms of mental illness." [1] If our external reality is desolate, it's hard to create a rich inner world. If we are creatively stimulated, our inner world becomes more complex. Fresh opportunities give us a chance to reshape our identity and discover new talents. When encouraged to play, many people manage to avoid burnout and find a new sense of joyfulness. Maintaining a balance between reality and imagination keeps us vital. Creativity and active imagining are part of our life force and, as such, need to be exercised.

In *Between Reality and Fantasy*, psychiatrist Gilbert Rose comments, "The critical gap across which the spark of life must pass has been pictured by Michelangelo as the vital space between the finger of the Creator and Man. This vital space sketches also the interval between individuation and fusion, self and other-ness. This is the arena for reality construction: the area of the transitional process." [2]

The equine program provides us with such an arena. Horses are a living story and a natural forum for blending reality with fantasy, fact with fiction, tragedy with comedy, and nature with the supernatural. They afford a positive, structured play form that appeals to our sense of accomplishment and aliveness. Within this forum, the mind and body join to set in motion a process of rejuvenation.

At the ranch we developed a way to play while exploring psychospiritual issues and giving birth to new opportunities. Using this approach, we're not as apt to resist change. In fact, we can get so involved in our play that our goal of changing becomes secondary to the pleasure we derive in the process we're going through. By letting go of our attachment to getting somewhere, a metamorphosis occurs spontaneously and effortlessly.

In order to play "well" we must develop, exercise and combine two capacities that we already have: healthy fantasy and spontaneity. Each of us is surrounded by endless potential for creating, but unless we have the desire, energy and ability to seize this bounty, it passes us by. The capacity to capture the moment while behaving responsibly—what we term disciplined play—is an important skill to acquire. Achieving it brings us vitality and success. With it, we can respond to old situations in new ways and respond adequately to new situations.

In spite of the obvious benefits of play, many of us have grown unaccustomed to playing. We find that we're too rigid and inhibited to play in a way that once came so easily to us. As we mature, we frequently lose touch with the proverbial inner child. Also, there are those who, as children, never really had the luxury to play.

To reintroduce people to play activity, we take them through a warm-up period that lets them ease into it and slowly relax their defenses. This warm-up opens the door to the unconscious and makes assimilation possible.

Preliminaries to Disciplined Play

Our first impressions of one another are very important in that they strongly influence the type of relationship we ultimately develop with that person. We're naturally cautious during initial encounters. However, if when we engage other people we reduce their uneasiness early on, they are more likely to become involved participants instead of outsiders.

The spirit with which we approach others is decisive in determining whether or not they decide to play with us. Our potential playmates must be challenged and intrigued but never threatened. It's up to us to find innovative ways to break the ice while maintaining social protocol.

Among nonhuman animals, initial familiarization between individuals is ceremonial and assumes a well-defined form. Herd animals, for example, are innately shy, reserved and formal during first encounters. A horse meeting another horse ritualistically moves forward and back, approaching then retreating. The retreating is as much a function of instinct as the approach. Until trust is established between the two animals, both postures are to be expected and respected.

It helps to think of ourselves in the same vein. Moving too quickly or too far without the proper, preliminary formalities causes alarm and raises defensive responses. Humans erect the same walls that animals do but in more subtle guises. For instance, the instant intimacy that was promoted during the 1960s proved to be detrimental in many cases, and the results were contrived, often obstructing true friendship and intimacy instead of promoting it.

It's important not to confuse formality with coldness. Formality simply means that there are rules to the game. By bringing our own authenticity, excitement and warmth to the situation, we establish an air of openness and help put one another at ease. We each get an opportunity to evaluate the other. When we genuinely enjoy the interchange, this gets communicated. When we can pique another's interest in us, the preliminaries have been successful.

Keeping interactions as natural as possible is especially important in making connections. It's also critical to keep in mind that, regardless of whom we're interacting with, that person must feel that he or she is in charge of his or her own destiny. Respecting individuals and giving them the power to decide if and when they want to open up lets them retain the reins of control.

The Power of Paradox

Life thrives because of the tension existing between opposing yet interdependent forces. The tension brings about change and, ultimately, a climax or resolution of the tension. This can be observed at the cellular level, where function depends upon the opposing processes of synthesis and degradation. This elemental cycle of buildup and breakdown is also a component of healthy productivity in an emerging self. Life and its associated problems constantly ebb and flow. Thus a seemingly insurmountable problem can lead to an unexpected and prosperous outcome, mistakes to new successes, death to renewal.

An effective means of working through a person's unyielding defenses is the use of paradox. Posing a paradox is curative in that it frees the mind from rigid constructs and helps us move with nature's rhythms. Hardships become avenues for change and obstacles become opportunities. This is how nature works. Yet few of us truly see this. In nature, disasters stimulate renewal. In spite of the human inclination to intervene and fix things, upheaval and turbulence literally keep the cycle of life moving.

Paradox serves a preparatory function in meditation, stress reduction, self-hypnosis or any other situation that requires us to interrupt old, repetitive patterns of thought and feeling. For example, some people who are learning to ride horses assume, for some reason, that they shouldn't be afraid. They try to hide their fear, with the result that the fear builds. Rather than encouraging them to fight it, we urge them to go with it. When they suppress their fear, they waste energy. When they address what they are feeling, they can focus on new things.

Working with paradox is illustrated in the cases of certain individuals who are chronically angry. In spite of their protestations to the contrary, such people unconsciously look to others to tell them to stop being angry so that they can rebel. Our approach to this person would be, "Why stop being angry? It may be the only thing that makes you feel alive."

Our client Paul was diagnosed as a chronic schizophrenic. Paul's delusions were so entrenched that he spent most of his time arguing, trying to prove to others that he existed and that his feelings were valid. Paul, an overweight young man, lived alone in a board-and-care home. He developed a habit of periodically dropping in at his local crisis center to report to the staff that he was starving. The staff members would try to deliver a dose of reality by saying something like, "You're not starving. You couldn't be. In fact you're somewhat overweight." Paul became irate, his anger flared, and soon he'd be screaming at the staff.

Shortly after we acquired Paul as a client, a crisis center staff worker called to ask us if we had any suggestions as to how to handle Paul's fits of rage. We suggested that they simply agree with his declarations that he was starving by stating, "Yes, you are starving for love and companionship." This brief statement quieted Paul. His delusion lost some of its strength and persistence, and Paul shifted his mental energy so that he could talk about things that were troubling him. He began to get his needs met in a more appropriate manner. Now he left the center feeling understood.

The paradox is a simple but potent tool that gets us unstuck by granting us permission to feel and think the unthinkable. Rather than ruminating over a problem in the same unproductive way, we gain new perspective. Because it speaks directly to the unconscious mind, bypassing the intellect, paradox is the basic element employed in hypnosis. In simplistic terms, paradox teaches the mind to focus by allowing it first to wander. This moves the mind toward a problem rather than away from it. This moving toward, in turn, promotes courage and confidence, whereas avoidance or flight only stimulates more fear. The paradox dilutes any fixation a person might have because one need not fight oneself constantly.

Because we are human, we are destined to ride the waves of life, which involves experiencing emotional as well as physical pain. Yet we often indulge ourselves in self-pity and feelings of helplessness, wasting energy by fighting the circumstances facing us. Life's unfairness is one of the most difficult truths we must face. Those who achieve this understanding have the opportunity to find boundless freedom. Those who continue to swim against the tide will drown in delusion and bitterness. The mind can be a magnificent ally or a ruthless enemy. We choose which it is to be.

The knowledge that life is paradoxical lets us shed the limitations imposed by our notion that life is either this or that. Instead, we learn that life is all of it. We begin to accept the wholeness of life and of ourselves. Paradoxically, when this happens, the paradox is resolved. To bring about this resolution, we must accept the goodness, the evil, and everything in between as part of who we are. There is nothing shameful in having dark sides to our hearts—we all do. The danger lies in choosing to become a creature of darkness rather than a bearer of light.

Educating the Unconscious Mind: Storytelling

Important shifts occur when we reach and educate the soul. Through storytelling, we touch not only the personal unconscious but the collective unconscious as well. Storytelling stretches the imagination and gives our minds more elasticity. Christ knew that the human soul could only be transformed indirectly and subliminally. He knew that when he told his parables, those who were ready for the message conveyed would grasp the true meaning and those who were not would simply attend to the literal content. Christ's parables were aimed at freeing us—psyche, spirit and soul—from our self-imposed hell. Through imagery and drama, the minds and hearts of his listeners took flight. Both fantasy and reality aroused the power of imagination in archetypal themes. Christ was among the first we know of who used guided imagery, hypnosis and psychodrama to engage participants in intrapsychic play.

Diverse forms of storytelling such as drama, dance, myth, literature and song have been used effectively throughout human history for problem-solving. Stories are also an excellent method of hypnosis. In *My Voice Will Go with You*, Sidney Rosen writes, "Since time immemorial stories have been used as a way of transmuting cultural values, ethics, and morality. A bitter pill can be swallowed more easily when it is embedded in a sweet matrix. A straight moral preachment might be dismissed, but guidance and direction become acceptable when embedded in a story that is intriguing, amusing, and interestingly told." [3] What hypnotist Milton Erickson understood, as did the ancients, was that to enter the unconscious in a benign way leads to change.

Weaning

Gail was a young woman in her 20s who was overly dependent on her mother. The relationship had become symbiotic. Gail often said she would rather die than leave home. Secretly, she feared separation would not only devastate her but her mother also. She considered the idea a betrayal that would kill both of them. Around this issue she was very sensitive and wanted to avoid any in-depth discussion of it.

She loved to sit and observe the horses on days when she would come to us for her therapy. One day she was actually present when a mare gave birth and said it was one of the finest and most sacred moments of her life. Out of curiosity and love, she followed the behavior of this mare and baby over the next six months. She saw the bonding process and the initial intensity of it, the mare being very active and protective, while instructing the foal was her sole ambition.

However, as the months passed, the foal would leave its mother's side for brief periods and play with the other foals in the field, as long as she remained within earshot and sight of the mare. These intervals became longer and longer. While the youngsters cavorted together, the mares congregated and socialized. Four months passed and the time for weaning came.

Mares typically adore their young and pour tremendous time and energy into their welfare. The most touching scene is seeing a foal sleep while its mother acts as sentry. Yet around weaning time, mares become tired and express a longing to be back in the company of adults. It is noticeable that they miss their own lives and friends. Most mares encourage their offspring to be outgoing and gregarious, knowing friendships and camaraderie are necessary to survival within the herd.

Since most mares are very secure in their mothering abilities, they also seem able to come to terms with the fact that, for now, the job of mothering is over. There is a brief sadness. It is a bittersweet occasion. At the initial shock of separation mother and young both cry, but usually for different reasons. Typically their grieving does not last for more than three days. Nonetheless, once separation has occurred, the mare never succumbs to the foal's regressive desires. She assumes the responsibility and ensures, by aggression if necessary, that the foal does not return to a dependent state. Mares are never ambivalent about this. They will recognize their progeny, glance at them with affection, but never let them nurse again. They also treat male and female offspring differently. After the weaning process has taken hold, females can live together. Like humans, some mothers and daughters get along well and become friends in adulthood, while others are diffident and hostile. In the case of males, mares are never friendly and foals must go their own way, someday to be stallions with their own herds of mares. This prevents incest within the herd and frees the mare for the next foal.

After months of observing this process, Gail came in, eager to talk in therapy. She blurted out, "I know what my problem is. I was never weaned properly." She had used the horse as a vehicle for self-exploration and had come to her own conclusions. She wanted her mother to come in so she could explain what she had learned and so both of them could understand this natural stage. Seeing the process from the horses' vantage point was nonthreatening; hence Gail and her mother were able to separate without guilt and hostility.

Educating the Unconscious Mind: Symbols

Symbols can also be used to spur personal growth. A person can be influenced deeply by representations while remaining unaware that transformation is taking place. Therefore, it's imperative that we expose ourselves to positive, growth-promoting symbols. Carl Jung discovered that people use symbols to communicate with one another in powerful ways on an unconscious level. In *Man and His Symbols*, Jung writes: "What we call a symbol is a term, a name, or even a picture that may be familiar in daily life, yet that possesses specific connotations in addition to its conventional and obvious meaning. It implies something vague, unknown or hidden from us. . . . Thus a word or an image is symbolic when it implies something more than the obvious and immediate meaning. . . . As the mind explores the symbol, it is led to ideas that lie beyond the grasp of reason. . . . Then there are certain events of which we have not consciously taken note; they have remained, so to speak, below the threshold of consciousness. They have happened, but they have been absorbed subliminally, without our conscious knowledge. We can become aware of such happenings only in a moment of intuition or by a process of profound thought that leads to a later realization that they must have happened; and though we may have originally ignored their emotional and vital importance, it later wells up from the unconscious as a sort of afterthought." [4] For example, one person may see a horse as a big four-legged animal, while another may see it as a noble conqueror.

The Mythic Horse

On a psychological level, the equine program takes the form of a quest, conjuring central motifs of the mythic journeys. As scholar Joseph Campbell pointed out, the purpose of myth is to teach us how to live. Myths help us overcome obstacles humans have always had to confront and conquer. Through fantastic imagery, myths instruct us on how to enlist the imagination to resolve age-old dilemmas.

One such mythic journey begins with an animal luring a person into a strange and unknown forest. In the course of the adventure, the dark forest becomes enchanted and the animal is transformed into God. Each traveler creates a personal story and plays the protagonist in it.

We once had a client—a successful career woman—who entered our program simply because she wanted more excitement in her life, an adventure of some sort. In addition to adventure, Susan said that she was also looking to achieve more balance in her life. She felt that at times she was overly serious and at other times too easily swept away. She was also highly self-critical. To ride horses had been Susan's childhood dream and something she felt would offer her a good challenge. She showed obvious talent in the arena, but her self-absorption got in the way.

As she progressed in the program, Susan seemed on the verge of forming a united team with the horse but for some reason couldn't quite achieve it. There was something mechanical about her presentation. As she continued her lessons, an interesting pattern came to our attention. Susan developed a disturbing tendency to give the horse too much rein one minute and too little the next. We noticed that as the horse became more animated and spirited, Susan's face became contorted, and she immediately clutched tightly at the left rein. Initially, we assumed this was simply a function of fear. Then we realized something more was going on.

One day, Susan came to her lesson and related a very detailed and elaborate dream she'd had the previous night. In it, Susan was a beautiful young girl who had just received a white horse for her birthday. She fell in love with this horse and promised to care for him. One lovely spring day, she and a new friend went for a ride in the hills, which were covered in wildflowers. Warmed by the sun, feeling overjoyed and full of herself, Susan decided, without consulting her horse, to keep on riding into the wind. On and on they traveled. When the horse became tired and thirsty, Susan became angry and impatient. She was having too much fun to stop. Even when the horse was ready to drop, she did stop but felt deep resentment.

As she lay in the grass pouting, Susan heard a loud, piercing cackle. Looking up, she saw a grotesque witch with a deformed claw hovering over her. Said the witch, "It's time to destroy you." Scared for her life, Susan leapt to her feet and turned to her horse, expecting it to turn away from her. To her surprise, the horse knelt and she mounted him easily. But the witch cast a spell so that the horse couldn't move. Turning to her horse, Susan pleaded, "I'm afraid. What should I do?" "Tell the witch you love her," replied the horse. As the words left her tongue, she and the horse took flight, soaring into the sky. Thinking she had made her escape, Susan was surprised to find the witch waiting for her. But this time, the witch sat beside a beautiful angel who said, "You have met my sister. Now that she has taught you to respect God, I will teach you how to play with God."

Shortly after having this dream, Susan stopped vacillating between overcontrolling the horse and overindulging him. She began to let the horse exercise his own spirit. She herself started using better judgment when it came to her own spirit and found some peace.

Each individual's quest is unique. The delinquent boys we work with learn about different aspects of the horse and horsemanship. We teach them the lore surrounding the horse in various world cultures. They learn of the *chevaliers* of France and the *caballeros* in Spain—esteemed and courageous men who adhered to strict codes of behavior and honor. The boys learn about the history of the Spanish *á la jineta* school of horsemanship that we use with our students. This traditional style is considered a sacred art. The colorful lore surrounding it, which is rich with lessons concerning community ethics and honor, has an impact on the young men who work with our horses.

For some, the horses fill a void by restoring their faith that goodness still exists in the world. In so many cases, the experience rekindles the capacity for feeling joy. The warmth derived from contact and working with the animals begins to overshadow inner desolation and rage in many of our program participants, and their sense of deadness and monotony subsides for the first time in many years. In short, the horses become beacons of hope, a sign that better days may lie ahead.

Elizabeth was 20 years old when we met her. She had been a model child, a straight-A student, an avid reader and a concert pianist. While growing up, there was little evidence that anything was wrong with her, except that she spent long hours isolated in her room. The piano was Elizabeth's only friend.

Although she was a lovely young woman, Elizabeth thought herself grotesquely ugly. She strongly believed that she lived under a curse and that her very presence endangered those loved ones around her. Elizabeth was suffering from schizophrenia.

As her disease progressed, Elizabeth grew more helpless and hopeless. Upon her return home from school one day, Elizabeth's older sister arrived to find her unconscious, lying in a pool of blood. Acting on impulse, Elizabeth had cut herself, believing self-sacrifice was necessary to spare her family from death. Elizabeth was in a delusional state when she was admitted to the hospital and was convinced that she had died and was now in hell.

When Elizabeth was referred to us for long-term treatment, we did not try to rid her of her delusions. Because we were more interested in earning her trust, we validated her feeling that she was, in fact, living in hell. We understood that she was simply trying to convey to the world exactly what she was experiencing. We did not doubt that her description was accurate.

Elizabeth's involvement with the horses made the delusion of hell increasingly difficult to sustain. Such loving animals would never reside in the devil's domain. Elizabeth began to question her perceptions.

One rainy day, the students asked to groom the horses inside the covered arena. Elizabeth went to get the gelding horse named Ensueño. As she opened the paddock to go out of the gate with the horse, she slipped, let go of the lead line and landed beneath the horse's feet. Terrified, the girl looked up at Ensueño and yelled, "Ensueño, Ensueño, please don't hurt me. Don't hurt me." Ensueño calmly lowered his large head to assure her she was safe, then slowly, carefully backed away and waited patiently for her to get up. Back on her feet, Elizabeth threw her arms around the horse and warmly thanked him for treating her so kindly and gently. Following this episode, her conviction that she was consigned to hell quickly dissolved. She knew without a doubt that Ensueño was one of God's creatures.

Planting the Seeds of Conscience

We speak of waves in a storm as "sea horses." Like wild horses, impetuous and irresistible, a man can drown in them, but if he can ride them in a well-founded ship (as a man rides a horse which carries him), they can support him on his voyages.

—John Layard, *A Celtic Quest: Sexuality and Soul in Individuation*

I n our view, conscience is the most important aspect of our psychological development. In psychological language or jargon it is called the "superego." It is the part of our psyche that humanizes us, giving us a capacity to feel for others, particularly love and compassion, and to live by certain ethics and principles.

When we have a well-developed conscience, the rules we live by are part and parcel of who we are, not externally imposed. People with a well-developed conscience know the difference between right and wrong, and try to do what is right. They are aware of others and care about the welfare of those with whom they are close.

Civility is another way of describing conscience that is characterized by a sense of humility and graciousness. When people are civil, they do not blame others if a problem arises and are more apt to realistically admit to their own strengths and weaknesses, having no need or desire to be perfect. Likewise, such individuals do not expect perfection from others. Most often, people with a conscience act responsibly and try to avoid hurting others.

The conscience, like any other psychological entity such as the "self" or the "ego," goes through stages and progresses to higher levels of sophistication, depending to a large degree on our environments and what has been expected of us.

What is it about horses that triggers such dramatic responses in people? How are they able to elicit such instantaneous respect and responsiveness? Our experience has taught us that it is the upheaval that horses are able to create in an individual's psyche. The upheaval can be experienced as something positive, making a lasting impression. It can also be felt as something negative, such as exposing hypocrisy or other embedded character flaws. Horses often trigger growth because they are so different from the pets people usually have in their lives, such as cats and dogs. We have to learn to relate in new ways.

Unlike most domesticated animals, horses quickly anchor us, making it difficult to escape from some of the basic realities of our existence. Around them we are confronted with existential truths and with matters of life and death, two of the most fundamental and pressing issues perplexing humankind. When dealing with horses, these issues are no longer remote. They become real and immediate. We begin to experience the death of our old ways of behaving and thinking.

Horses are capable of stimulating great excitement and joy as well as awakening feelings of vulnerability and fallibility. Situating us between these two polarities becomes a powerful catalyst for human growth. Horses are commanding in size and their impressive spirit, an attention-grabber. In their company we can get hurt, through our own lack of experience or awareness, ignorance or provocation. Additionally, when we ride them we can, literally, fall.

By confronting these human fears head-on and at some point mastering them, we gain more courage to brave life. Becoming more contemplative and philosophical in the process, we are no longer so apt to take the gift of life for granted. By contrast, running away from fear, as we humans tend to do, undermines our spiritual development. Facing these realities doesn't change what we have to cope with in life, but it teaches us to make the transitions more gracefully.

Master equestrians have known for centuries that horses can teach us how to maximize our own human virtues, if we allow them. They have a unique talent for extracting, exposing and edifying defects in our individual characters, which is difficult to do for ourselves. Thus, we emerge from the experience with a great sense of accomplishment and renewal. Therefore, when humans ultimately manage to make a safe and loving relationship with a horse, the intimacy fairly won feels exhilarating, like jumping a big psychic hurdle.

Knowing Oneself

Many years ago a woman who was a dilettante visited the ranch. She was very glamorous and loved to live in the fast lane, going to parties, carousing with men and dabbling in drugs. Catherine couldn't fathom the idea of communing with nature. Solitude was something outside of her paradigm. Not having a function or event to attend on a regular basis made life boring.

Catherine bragged about her escapades and *savoir faire*. However, the lifestyle she described and flaunted sounded more like living on the edge. Flirting with danger on more than one occasion, she was known to do self-destructive things and to put herself in marginal situations, particularly with men who had a good facade and excellent earning power and credentials but who were abusive to her.

Catherine could be arrogant and rubbed many people the wrong way. If anything hindered her in life, it was this trait.

However, for the most part she was unaware of the effect her arrogance had on other people. She couldn't "clean up her act" because she didn't know, or feel, she had one. The expression, "she didn't know she didn't know," fit her unconscious style of living.

Catherine originally came to visit our horses more out of competition and curiosity than anything else. She had heard about them through a woman friend who had seen us performing at a charity event. Urbanized to the core, it was obvious Catherine wasn't interested in the country or the horses, only in outdoing her friend. Upstaging others and gaining a heightened sense of status was a driving motivation in her life. Despite all her pretenses, we could sense Catherine wasn't very happy. Since her friend signed up for lessons, she wanted to as well.

The first day with Catherine was memorable. She prided herself on knowing horses and said, "I am not afraid. I could be in a herd of stampeding horses and it wouldn't bother me." It sounded good, but it wasn't real. Questioning her further, we learned she had ridden casually at various public stables. However, she saw herself as some kind of expert.

After her first lesson, she asked to ride one of our young stallions. Interestingly, she was in need of some kind of domination over males in general. What she couldn't do in life she would now try to do with the horses. By and large, we do not let inexperienced people ride stallions. Riding stallions can be very tricky, requiring the most expertise, knowledge and intuition. Most people sense instinctually that it is best to stick to riding well-schooled geldings and mares, unless you are really competent. When we tried to explain this to her, she wouldn't listen. We didn't argue with her because it wouldn't have done any good. We learned a long time ago in the psychotherapy business that giving advice and being a do-gooder is a waste of time. As a rule of thumb, most of us seldom take advice—we have to learn the hard way.

So when she came back to ride, still insisting, we allowed her to walk one of the stallions from his paddock up to where we saddle horses. Peruvian stallions, by nature, are typically very tractable, learning to be noble via a process of education. By way of socialization, like children, they learn to be attentive, considerate and respectful, and to control their impulses in the presence of people.

Lacking any real in-depth horse experience, Catherine was unaware of how young stallions naturally behave. As she walked by a large paddock full of young mares, one was in heat. The young stallion, not knowing or respecting Catherine, went up on his hind legs and made lots of noise. He was not trying to hurt her but was excited. Faced with the reality of a horse standing above her head on his two hind legs was intimidating to say the least. She called for help. Catherine not only came down to earth but started to listen to us.

Of her own volition, she decided that handling and riding a stallion were beyond her present skills. She also elected to stick with even-tempered geldings and mares until she had more savvy. Awestruck by the powerful nature of the stallion's energy, she began to talk more realistically about her own abilities. No longer denying her fear and dangerous level of naiveté, she became more sensible, recognizing without having to be told that if she were truly an expert, she would have been prepared and able to handle this young stallion. The horse forced Catherine, by eliciting fear, to question herself. She began asking questions: "How often in life do I bite off more than I can chew?" "How often do I get

myself into situations that I am unequipped to handle?"
"What is my driving need to dominate male animals?"

Catherine began to act differently after this confrontation.
She continued with the horse program. As time went on, she
also developed more inner substance. The better she felt
about her own abilities, the less she used men for prestige. In
the process, she reexamined some of her values and priorities
in life. She didn't change overnight, but it was a start.

Popular wisdom notwithstanding, this upheaval is invaluable. It lays down the rudiments of conscience and reminds us
of our humanity. Complacency keeps us stagnant, leaving us
no chance for redemption. Riding horses also places us in a
state of vulnerability. When we are on their backs, depending
on them, the control is out of our hands.

Jane was going though midlife crisis. As she entered
menopause, she was acting more and more adolescent. She
had an inner desire to live out a youthful fantasy of owning
a horse.

This fantasy in and of itself is not unhealthy. In fact, in
many cases, it signals stability and maturity. Typically, the
childhood fantasy reoccurs in people over 40 who have
worked very hard and want more adventure in life. The idea
typically reemerges as a result of success. It is an excellent
opportunity for families. The individual now has the means to
afford the fantasy about which he or she could once only
dream. However, in Jane's situation the fantasy emerged for
different reasons. It was a desperate attempt on her part to
avoid and deny the realities of growing older.

Despite her husband's words of caution, Jane was bound
and determined. She went out and purchased a horse without
background or experience. Jane found a mare that had all the

characteristics and qualities that Jane herself felt she was losing: youth, beauty, energy and bravado. The mare was also a gorgeous palomino with a long and luxurious mane and tail.

We originally met Jane during her quest to find the "perfect" mare. Since we are an educational center, she came to talk to us at her husband's insistence. However, her heart wasn't in it; it was only a gesture to appease him. We told her to do her homework. Buying a horse for color or length of mane is a big mistake many people make—and regret later. Nevertheless, she was determined to find a "blond beauty" and didn't want to hear anything that might sway her.

Not knowing horses, but familiar with dogs and cats, she assumed they were all the same. After a two-year search she finally found the "right" mare. Not only did the mare fit her ideal, but she was also saddle-trained. However, as a beginner swept away by her enthusiasm, Jane had failed to ask one pertinent question: What level of rider is this mare trained to carry? Since the mare was easy to handle on the ground, Jane took it for granted she would be the same under saddle. Jane was ecstatic. She had daydreams of their rides together, going to the beach, walking though beautiful meadows. She took excellent care of the horse and did all the right things.

Thinking they had made a relationship, Jane decided to go on a trail ride for the first time and enjoy the vistas. The ride wasn't what Jane had expected: it was frightful. The mare was hot as a pistol and very headstrong. Jane walked the mare back on foot, not telling a soul. Instead of acknowledging her fear and the problem, she rationalized it away, convincing herself that the mare was acting up because she didn't know Jane well enough. On the contrary, the mare knew Jane very well. As we've seen time and again, horses know each of us inside and out the minute we enter their territory or sit on their backs. It takes them only a few seconds to get a fix on who we are.

Jane's remedy was to coddle the mare. As she stated later, "I thought if I showered her with lots of unconditional love we would bond and get closer." This is the same mistake many parents make with their own children. Instead of earning their children's respect, they try to bribe them by being nice. In this case, the parents' need to be liked overrides the child's need to be disciplined. In dealing with both horses and people, this solution is a classic formula for trouble. Jane fell into this trap. She continued to pamper the mare for six more months, secretly hoping she would be able to ride and control her.

Jane's plan backfired and the situation went from bad to worse. The next time she tried riding the mare, instead of just running away with Jane, she started bucking and wheeling. Jane fell off and had to face some cold hard facts. This mare was too much for her to handle.

In assessing this mare, it was clear she was spoiled and used to getting her own way. She did not respect human beings and, for the most part, did not even acknowledge their existence. When they interfered in her plans, she would try to bully them by being explosive. This horse was not bonded to anyone; in fact, she found nothing pleasurable about humans. Her sole ambition under saddle was to get them off her back. Whether her obstinate character originated from physical pain, injury or psychic problems was hard to determine at this stage. However, we suspect all three were at play, resulting in her sour and defiant attitude.

Jane's bubble had burst. However, what eventually became clear to her was that she had, in fact, picked the perfect mare. Unconsciously, she selected a mare who would teach her the

most about the dark side of her own personality. What originally seemed like a curse to Jane turned into a godsend, making her wiser and more discerning.

Every time she rode the mare she was riding herself and had
to contend with her own willfulness: she and the mare were
identical in this respect. Both liked to take charge of situations, be bossy and not listen to anyone. They used their
energy to resist rather than move forward. Jane had met her
match, yet the mare, being bigger and stronger, was able to
outdo her. Jane was humbled. The mare was successful in disrupting Jane's status quo.

In the course of retraining the mare, Jane also learned some
important life lessons. Since her own character was brought
out into the open by a horse she had handpicked, she had no
one to blame except herself. In this situation, getting angry
would have been futile. Instead, she began to reflect on her
behavior and reevaluate some things.

Affecting Others

Not only do horses produce upheaval in humans, but we
can evoke it in them as well. Awareness of how deeply we can
affect them shakes us to the core. A successful financier
owned a multiprize-winning national champion stallion.
Doug adored this horse. Every night after work, weather per-
mitting, he and his stallion, Mario, would ride into the hills
and unwind. They had many wonderful times together.

After years of owning this stallion, Doug and his wife began
having marital problems. His wife of 20 years decided she
didn't want to be a housewife anymore. She wanted out of the
marriage "to find herself." She was going to live in Mexico

with a friend. Her decision hit Doug like a ton of bricks. He was beside himself. His life on all fronts began to suffer.

In the throes of divorce he became very depressed, blaming himself for the situation. He became so preoccupied he was unable to spend ample time, as he had in the past, with his dear friend Mario. Although Doug ensured Mario was well cared for by his ranch workers, it wasn't the same. Mario missed their rides together terribly.

As the divorce proceedings progressed, things between Doug and his wife became worse. His wife demanded liquidation of many of their assets because she wanted cash so she could travel. In her eyes, Mario was just another lucrative asset. She asked her attorney to insist the court sell Mario as part of the settlement. Doug couldn't handle this demand.

As the sale became more and more imminent, he went into an emotional tailspin. Not only was he losing his wife but also his companion Mario. Instead of facing the dilemma and confronting his pain in a different way, Doug withdrew completely. Feeling sorry for himself, he went to work, but aside from that he stopped seeing everyone, including Mario.

Mario was never sold because he died first. This young, healthy and robust horse suddenly died of colic. We often wonder if death was Mario's way out of a heartbreaking, no-win situation. Doug wonders too. He has had to examine the negative effect of his own self-indulgence.

In practicing therapy in a wide range of settings with an equally diverse client population, and working with horses, we have come to change some long-held ideas about what is healthy for the human organism. Upheaval, fear and discomfort are not only useful in taming aggression at various stages of our personal development, but are vital aspects of existence.

To experience those rare but welcome feelings of insight and ecstasy, we must also learn to endure transient periods of upset and fear. This notion may seem strange in a society that always wants to be comfortable.

Facing Fear

In recent years, the trend in our culture has been to contrive to avoid experiencing fear altogether. We have increasingly insulated ourselves from even the awareness of our vulnerability. While as a society we've achieved an unprecedented level of material comfort, we're witnessing more antisocial behavior and a higher occurrence of psychopathology. The more we shield ourselves from realistic fears of death, disease, natural disaster, et cetera, the more widespread this human pathology will become. Safe within our technological cocoon, we are acquiring a dangerous form of arrogance. Without a healthy reverence for life's fragility, we take existence for granted and, in cases of psychopathology, desecrate it.

Physiologically, human beings are designed to experience short-lived bouts of fear that trigger in us adaptive responses to situations. Occasionally, the fear-response mechanisms need to be activated so that we can survive. Recent research shows that a momentary experience of fear bolsters the immune system by stimulating the buildup of killer cells that help fight off disease. Short-lived fear also stimulates the secretion of hormones like adrenaline that enhance our physiological and behavioral responses to threat. Protracted fear, however, results in physical exhaustion and breakdown.

The beneficial character of fear holds true on a psychological level as well. Periods of fear and anxiety are necessary components of personal health and growth. People who experience little or no anxiety about their (or another's) problems are usually poor candidates for traditional psychotherapy because they don't feel the problems are their responsibility. They will habitually shift blame to others. These jolts of fear open the door to deeper feelings. In treating such clients, the therapist has to impose anxiety from an external source. The therapist does this by reminding clients about present reality— something clients may prefer to forget. Horses naturally induce these fleeting but normal surges of anxiety.

For some clients, a healthy dose of reality focuses their attention on the gravity of their situation. For others, it has no noticeable impact. Substance abusers typify this latter group. They may seek treatment only after they've hit rock bottom and their families and/or friends insist that they get help. However, hitting rock bottom or listening to family members may take years. Horses have a way of speeding up the process. A swift kick from a horse is something an individual is more apt to feel and remember. The message—being direct and potent—penetrates defenses, particularly denial. Others may have more benign life-skill problems, such as poor work performance or inability to get along with other people. In these cases, individuals play the role of victim, transferring responsibility for their problems onto others, coming to therapy in response to an ultimatum. Still others in this category come for help of their own volition, but often it's in the hope of learning new tactics for getting their own way, rather than a tool for self-discovery. Once that mission is accomplished and they obtain whatever they were looking for, self-exploration ends and they will probably quit therapy. With horses, people are less likely to play these habitual games because it doesn't bring relief. When people blame the horse, which many do, it doesn't solve the problem—it only makes it worse. The only way a horse will cooperate and forgive is if we look at our own part in the problematic interaction.

People who are experiencing some kind of psychological pain have the best chance of using the help extended to them and improving their situations. Unfortunately, we've all been programmed to think of pain, generally, as a bad thing. When we encounter a friend who's depressed or afraid, we automatically try to take that distress away and to cheer the person up. While we may be operating with the best of intentions, this Band-Aid approach only reinforces the condition. Unless people experience their pain completely and begin to understand it, they will not only fail to overcome it, they'll also lose the opportunity of using it to advance their own growth. Pain can get you somewhere, and that somewhere can be a life-enhancing experience.

We all tend to forget that pain can signal change. Alleviating the symptoms of pain in someone, without helping them to get at its underlying source, robs them of an important tool for self-exploration. It's also a way of placating that reinforces the person's need to cave in and succumb to another. This attitude undermines healthy character development and contributes to psychospiritual, moral and, ultimately, social decay.

By comparison, horses operating by the laws of nature only do what they feel is just. Each response is usually in direct proportion to what the individual person needs or deserves. They are not constricted as we humans are by sentimentality or political correctness. They are creatures that will not indulge our character weaknesses. Although they may feel empathy toward us, they rarely feel sympathy.

In examining the state of moral deterioration so prevalent in our culture, we begin to suspect that the level of security we've achieved is the primary culprit. The word "security" originates from the Latin *sin-cura*, which means to be free from death's messenger. Perhaps protecting ourselves from the reality of death isn't such a good thing. Although most people in our society are inclined to shy away from the subject of their own death, this has not always been the case. Previously, through a variety of acceptable outlets such as ritual and tradition and religious, literary, or artistic disciplines, people were given constructive avenues to explore and deal with death. These activities helped us gain a greater sense of inner peace and understanding. Confronting what scares us the most usually results in mastery. Flight accelerates the fear, making it seem larger and more ominous than it really is.

Facing the Death Experience

Those who've had a near-death experience have been changed profoundly by it and have acquired a more universal consciousness. Their lives take on new depth and meaning, and they feel a stronger sense of direction and purpose. However, it's not necessary to have a near-death experience to face the issue of mortality. Death and resurrection are all around us. Powerful images like the Classic Horse shake the psyche and ignite a process of contemplation, leading to symbolic forms of rebirth.

This happened to Bill, a teenage boy who had been in one of our residential treatment homes. When admitted to our program, he immediately gravitated to the horses. The love he felt for them abated his chronic desire to run away and use drugs. He even lost interest in his former street activities.

While in the program he showed such talent with the horses that we let him work with a gelding who was difficult to school. The horse wasn't mean; he just had his own ideas about things. So Bill set out on this project to fine-tune the horse. He poured his heart and soul into educating the horse, gently and with finesse. Within four months, he and the horse were moving together like clockwork, executing beautiful turns, doing serpentines, stopping with a light touch, backing straight. They were both involved and loving every minute of their time together.

Then we got a call from Bill's social worker. Bill's mother, without any prior warning, had decided she was moving back to Chicago. Although she was an addict and a prostitute, the court had given her custody, and she demanded that Bill go with her. He was devastated. His life became black again, and he lost all hope for his future. He sank into deep despair. There were many tearful good-byes, especially between Bill and the gelding. We lost contact with him, but six years later we received a card from him saying he was in jail for dealing drugs. He had been doing some serious thinking and thought he was ready to turn around. He wanted to know how our horses were. He told us that remembering the gelding he had worked with had brought him out of his anger and rage, that one day in his jail cell he had begun to have memories of the horse that he had suppressed. He said the horse just kept reappearing.

While Bill was in jail we sent him the horse literature and Peruvian and Spanish horse magazines he requested. He studied everything he could get his hands on while finishing his time. Recognizing how foolish he had been, when he got out he enrolled in a junior college. In reexamining his life, he figured out he needed to get a college education and a good-paying job to own a horse of his own some day. It was this dream that spurred him on and kept him motivated. He finished college and became a teacher.

Between Two Worlds

Whether we encounter death vicariously through stories and symbols or in actuality, exposure to it enlightens us. The awareness gained helps transform our law-and-order-based mentality to a more inclusive and conscious morality. This occurs because we move into a realm of the unknown where there are no hard-and-fast rules. Death being the ultimate mystery, we seldom get a glimmer of what's behind the curtain. Therefore, when we do, it leaves a profound and transforming effect.

We grasped this concept at an even deeper level when Grandmother died. Grandmother was also an avid horsewoman, making three generations of horse aficionados. When she turned 90, she insisted on riding a horse one last time. After that, she was content to watch and supervise the rest of us. Even into her mid-90s she would sit in the paddocks of various horses and talk to them. Grandmother took great comfort in animals, and as long as we can remember, animals had always been her companions and confidantes. Fortunately, she had them to turn to after she had outlived most of her family and friends. We firmly believe her experience with animals—particularly the horses she knew—set the stage for her dignified acceptance of death.

The following account—in Marlena Deborah's own words —illustrates very personally the turbulent and transforming nature of death, what can happen when we remove our pre-conceived notions and allow nature to take its course. We write about it here because it affected us so significantly—not only triggering in us a quest for greater spirituality but also an increased desire to learn about the secrets of nature and the thriving world that surrounds us. This experience made us stop and think.

Grandmother's exemplary courageousness taught us about life and, ultimately, about death. She died at 97 years of age in a convalescent home that she had entered for medical rea-sons just four months previously. Prior to that, she'd insisted on living independently in her own home.

Until very near the end of her life, Grandmother lived expansively and with great gusto. Her iron will, which was evident to the last, impressed upon us the fact that we die as we have lived. When at last she entered the nursing home, she asked us to bring in Mac, our Jack Russell terrier, to see her. He represented the living spark that connected her to nature. When she died, he was lying at the foot of her bed.

By the time she arrived at the convalescent home, a place for the terminal or those close to death, she had made up her mind to die and prepared herself for this transition. During this crossing-over period, many questions arose for her and for us, including, Is it death we're really afraid of, or is it life? During the long hours at her bedside, Grandmother took us with her on her travels to the other side, to the light and the realm of the dead.

During one visit, I suddenly felt that I had entered a place of forgotten souls. The vibrancy was astonishing, with strong and resounding voices around me. "In the name of the Father, the Son and the Holy Spirit. Amen. Let God be with you and also with you." I looked around at the withered, weatherbeaten faces, the shriveled hands, the frail bodies, and felt an overwhelming sense of calm. I was no longer in a house of death but a sacred house of transition, of preparation. Time stood still and the decrepit, pained bodies seemed poised toward freedom.

Then Grandmother took me by the hand and said, "Debbie, you have got to get me out of here. Take me out of here. I want to go home now." As she pleaded with me, the words continued to echo within me: "Let God be with you and also with you." Speaking again with increasing desperation, Grandmother said, "You have got to get me out of this hell."

I could hardly bear the feelings this brought up in me. I understood her longing for the warmth of the sun, the birds' songs, the animals at play, and especially her horse. She felt her passionate affair with nature slipping from her. I felt I was betraying her but, because of her medical condition, I could not take her home.

Although at 97 she was still quite with it mentally, Grandmother's body was playing tricks on her. I studied the hollow cheeks of this once glamorous woman and wondered quietly whether she was a dying body or an angel. Her mental acuity contrasted sharply with her physical state and made her advanced age seem all the more painful. Sensing that her life was fading, I simply held her hand. "I'm going home," she informed me. "Times have changed and I've nowhere else to go. There is no place in the world for an old lady like me." I had to laugh because she'd always been such a realist. Yet, as she spoke, I was feeling some of the same things she was expressing—Times have changed. Where do I belong?—and I was overcome with terror. She was leaving and I still had the rest of my life ahead of me. I felt profoundly sad. I loved her so much and would miss this ancient one a great deal.

During the vigil, I lost track of time. Within a week, Grandmother was failing. In the throes of death, she called out to those who had gone before her, experiencing a grand reunion. "George, Catherine, Mama, Mama." She had reached my grandfather, her favorite long-deceased sister and her own beloved mother. Although she was drawn toward them, she still reached out to me, to the living. "Hello, dear. Take care of yourself."

Then another, more powerful presence beckoned Grandmother. With more force than I thought she had in her, she yelled, "God yes. Oh God yes. Yes, God, take me with you. I will go with you." She turned to me again, squeezed my hand and said, "I love you. I see Sonora. She is as beautiful as ever and is waiting for me. Look, do you see her? She is there. I must not keep her waiting." Sonora was an old mare that Grandmother would sit and talk to at our ranch. They would reminisce of days gone by, when both could leap and dance. Grandmother shared all her fears and joys with Sonora. They would spend hours together, Sonora nuzzling her while Grandmother sat in her favorite chair in Sonora's paddock. What we didn't know at the time, and neither did Grandmother, was that Sonora had been taken home by a friend she belonged to and had died of old age.

Grandmother was simultaneously situated in two worlds. Weak and emaciated, she turned and spoke to me with the same conviction she'd always had. "Come on, dear, let's go out for a walk now. I'm going home." These were the last words she uttered.

A true romantic to the last, Grandmother died on Valentine's Day, embarking on her journey home with renewed anticipation and hope. She would be with family and her beloved horses. As her soul took flight I realized that what the Divine gives, no one can take away. What God gives us is spirit. This kernel of light strengthens us and supplies us with the courage to meet our problems head-on and with meaningful perspective. Therefore, we need to nurture this spirit—the divine disorder that makes us complete—to exercise it wisely and, most of all, to cherish it as the treasure it is.

Moral Development

During the initial stages of moral development, fear and upheaval are the salient variables that keep our asocial behavior in check. Soon thereafter we begin to abide by externally imposed rules in order to avoid being punished. However, to go beyond a conscience that needs outside control, we need to remind ourselves of our own mortality. Potential peril and death are necessary ingredients for an internalized conscience. They instill in us an unparalleled reverence for life and remind us of our priorities and of what we have in common with each other.

Someone who has achieved a higher level of moral development has usually gone through some form of rebirth and emerged emptied of hate and with strong feelings regarding the sanctity of life, more concerned with the spirit of the living and less distracted by personal minutiae. This person behaves with civility not because it is necessary but because to do otherwise would be a violation of self and personal ideals. Knights in the chivalric tradition epitomized advanced moral development, thus making the Grail legends so inspiring.

Ideals are internally generated rather than externally imposed. Were we to receive Ten Commandments based on personal ideals, they would read differently from those that we know. Because our ideals are the products of our innermost thoughts and feelings, they provide a window into the soul. The recognition of our mortality helps us reconnect with our ideals.

The peoples of ancient civilizations understood that an awareness of death, gained through the experience of potential peril, is a pathway to life. The idea was not to put oneself at unnecessary risk but to face the real trials of everyday life. This rite of passage moves us through our fear of death and instills in us a reverence for life. Observing clients involved in the equine program has shown us that when people feel a certain amount of apprehension and anxiety, they gravitate toward one another and begin to appreciate the importance of being part of a community. This is true for everyone.

Although the exact nature of the trials varies according to the era in which we live, when we experience them, we begin to look beyond ourselves to the divine for clarity and comfort. Ancient Egyptians looked to the sun god—represented by the symbolic Sun Eye, the vigilant god—for protection, guidance and salvation. For the ancient Greeks, Helios, the god of the sun, was the eye in the sky. It was he who brought that which is concealed into light.

In equine therapy, horses serve the role of eye in the sky— the powerful, all-seeing witnesses that bring light into the darkness. They reflect back our fear/anxiety, which can ultimately stimulate development of an internalized sense of accountability and conscience. This comes about through the transformation of our perceptions of the horse into a creature with extraordinary teaching powers. Horses have the power to see through us. We are only and completely human in their presence—nothing more and nothing less. They accept us as we are, even when our fellow human beings don't.

When we work within this dimension, we experience a heightened sense of importance and expand our capabilities. With their keen powers of observation and vision, horses see behind our public personae. They see beyond our physical fear and sense our fear of being exposed. Horses quickly uncover who we are. Belief in the power of a being outside ourselves plants the seeds of respect from which conscience arises. This respect lies at the root of our capacity to care for something outside ourselves and is the developmental fore-runner of humility, reverence and deep love.

In a metaphorical sense, we need the polarities of darkness and light, of good and evil, to remain charged. To become aware of both our positive and negative sides opens many doors and keeps us physically and mentally balanced. The challenge is to work with these polarities and face the stark realities that each holds.

10 Spirituality

Creative work thus may be said to have a dual role: at the same time as it enlarges the universe by adding or uncovering new dimensions, it also enriches and expands man, who will be able to experience these dimensions inwardly. It is committed not just to the visible but, in many cases, to the invisible as well. Indeed, it is the perennial (and almost always unverbalized) premise of creativity, to show that the tangible, visible, and audible universe is infinitesimal in comparison to the one that awaits discovery through exploration of the external world and of the human psyche. A new painting, poem, scientific achievement, or philosophical understanding increases the numbers of islands of the visible in the ocean of the unknown.

—Silvano Arieti, *Creativity: The Magic Synthesis*

Self-realization is the most effective avenue we have for exploring and strengthening a spiritual identity. It provides us strong footing with which to travel into the recesses of heart and mind. Reaching these nether regions, which are characterized by raw energy, irrationality and chaos, is imperative because it rounds out our life experience and gives fuller access to the soul. These aspects of our psyche are sometimes collectively referred to as our animal mind. By contrast, the ego, the domain of consciousness, abides by the tenets of logic, convention and order. Naturally, these two provinces often operate at cross-purposes. To be complete, we need to unify these polarized factions and draw on the resources of both. This unification will enable us to live productive lives while embracing a larger cosmic vision.

We need to develop a mediating entity capable of integrating the divergent rational and animal parts of our nature. Jung referred to such an entity as the "self." The goal of individuation is to find this self. In the process of individuation we become not only whole but also holy. (The word "holy" is derived from the Greek *hagios*, which translates literally as "to be separate or set apart.")

As we discover inner truths, character is shaped and individuality forms. When this happens, we cease being conformists. Instead of blindly adhering to externally imposed ideology and mores, we tap into a higher, innate intelligence and turn inward for our direction. The core of our being is a mystical place that is the source of our inner voice and pure intuition. This powerful voice of wisdom is our connection to the divine. Within this sanctuary lies also our creative self, which helps us find novel and ethical solutions to our most horrific difficulties. Self-realization gives birth to new levels of consciousness and marks the advent of spirituality.

In Search of a Creative Core

If we are courageous enough to look directly into our own souls and confront our imperfections without self-condemnation, we'll find ourselves on a metaphysical path. When we can sustain compassion for ourselves as well as others, in the face of naked truth, we can open to divine inspiration and intervention. When this happens, the world no longer feels polarized into good versus evil, male versus female, or life versus death. The divisive internal battle stops and the world simply is. Instead of analyzing, idealizing, or trying to control natural processes, one simply watches, listens and receives what the world has to teach. The acceptance of life in its totality signifies transformation and the capacity to experience the oneness of which everything is a part. This shift is frequently accompanied by a spiritual awakening, a new sense of a universal force, or whatever one chooses to call it.

There has been a trend recently in some popular literature to divide and polarize God into male and female components. In nature, assignation of gender to God, or the Creator, is not an issue. Creation begins with the marriage, rather than the divorce, of male and female principles. This union gives rise to forgiveness, the merciful quality that allows us to see beyond flaws to the beauty and worth in existence. Through compassion and forgiveness we can learn the true meaning of faith, love and fellowship. When we overcome our narcissism, our bodies can learn to play and our hearts begin to dance.

Although involvement in various religious and mystical practices holds the opportunity for spiritual enrichment, so do most of our own day-to-day-experiences that we take for granted. Through incorporating horses into the therapeutic setting, we found a bridge between earthly, "mundane" activity and the mystical—and an avenue for spiritual development that would be closer to home. Home is, after all, where we have to spend our lives and practice our spirituality.

The Creative Spirit

The concept of awakening an inner living spirit feels foreign to many people because it hasn't been a primary focus of our materialistic culture. In other parts of the world a mystical or spiritual thread is woven into the very fabric of everyday life. Most Americans have been raised to see spirituality as something one might devote a few hours to on the weekend. We tend to view it more as a lifestyle option than a fact of life.

Cultivating ourselves as spiritual beings starts with integrating all of our feeling levels. When we have free access to all our feelings, we free ourselves from internal conflicts that inhibit spiritual growth. The energy we previously expended on conflict then becomes available for fueling our creative endeavors. Although we seldom actually stop to consider the creative force within us, we depend upon this most vital human resource to mine our full potential.

A central theme running through history, myth and fantasy is the existence within the universe of a force that is available to all of us. Quantum physics substantiates this claim. Scientists tell us that matter as we think of it does not actually exist—only dynamic energy. Our living human energy is in constant exchange with, and indeed is a part of, this universal energy. We have the capacity to help direct this exchange, strengthening our spirits in the process. By amplifying our inner vibrations, we can increase our strength and presence. In the field of physics, this growth-promoting force is called energy.

For centuries, mystics from Eastern as well as Occidental traditions have postulated that humans are pulsating energy systems who, through the use of spiritual tools, can develop advanced powers. In *The Secret Life of Plants*, Peter Tompkins and Christopher Bird address the correspondence between these long-held tenets and current scientific thought. "That plants, as well as animals and human beings, have fields of fine sheaths of subatomic or protoplasmic energy which permeate the solid physical bodies of molecules and atoms was a centuries-old allegation by seers and philosophers."[1] In art and literature, the attainment of superconsciousness has historically been depicted as saintly persons emitting halos or auras. For this reason, parapsychologists look to auras to obtain information about someone's spiritual essence and general well-being.

Passion

Passion springs from an innate energy, known simply to most of us as the will to live, and originates from our basic survival instincts. This pulse of life not only sustains us but, properly nurtured, can metamorphose into heightened creativity, animation and an indescribable sense of vibrancy.

The word "passion" comes from the Latin *pati*, meaning "to suffer." So, to feel passion in its fullest sense implies embracing life as it is, with all its darkness and pain. Through suffering, we open our hearts and minds, as the saints are said to have done, to the whole of living rather than some limited fantasy of how we think it should be. Experiencing passion keeps us from developing tunnel vision. The spiritual teacher Krishnamurti wrote, "Understanding really is passion; without passion you can't do anything. Intellectual passion is not passion at all. But to examine the whole of living needs not only extraordinary clarity of perception, but also the intensity of passion."[2] By understanding our multifaceted human character we discover many dimensions within as well as outside us. Rudolf Steiner wrote, "In short, when we experience this ebb and flow of destructive and beneficent forces in us for a time—then we will become more and more mature in our self-knowledge. . . . Observing our own coming into being and dying away is the first stage of true self-knowledge."[3] Through this retreat inward we begin to understand the peaks and valleys we call living.

In modern discussion, the idea of passion is often invoked only within the context of two instincts—sex and aggression—or confused with restlessness and hysteria. This limited and distorted view appears to stem from a voracious appetite for arousal. As a culture, we're seeking ever-increasing levels of excitement in order to feel alive. Collectively, we've pushed our tolerance threshold for stimulation to dangerously high levels. Anything less produces boredom. The violent and sexually charged content of our popular music, film and television programming mirrors this escalated need for arousal. Commercial technology now offers us computer-generated experiences as substitutes for living. It is now possible to commit "virtual" murder.

This phenomenon is indicative of a dearth of passionate feeling within us. The preoccupation with emotions versus feelings has also contributed to the creation of a society of ungrounded thrill seekers. Violence, with its concomitant lack of passion and compassion, is a natural consequence of the carelessness with which we tend to our spirit.

By tapping into our instinctual reserves, we can deliberately and consciously unearth a spiritual gold mine. Horses in particular embody this spirit, and can teach us how to productively use our animal minds and release their energy in responsible ways. Working with these ethereal yet grounded creatures generates natural excitement and facilitates spiritual opening.

The Creative Process: Becoming a Centaur

Years ago we participated in a horse festival that had been organized as a fund-raising event. Many breeds and riding styles were represented. A number of *dressage* experts were there, essentially performing ballet on horseback. One rider in particular caught our attention at the festival. This man, who was atop a magnificent white stallion, looked as though he'd just walked out of the pages of a history book. Rider and horse were both clad in Portuguese bullfighting costumes. Their performance was completely captivating.

Like other riders, they were performing very advanced "high school" movements. But apart from the expert technical level of their maneuvers, there was something special about this man and horse. Their performance had a brilliance, an ethereal quality to it that the others, in spite of their polish, lacked. They performed as one, like the centaur, the mythical Greek race of men who were half horse in their bodies and in their natures. We learned that the rider was an old-style master of the Classical Latin school of *dressage*, which prides itself on capturing the spirit of the horse through movement. We decided to investigate this ancient school of horsemanship further.

We continued to study with different experts who specialized in this method of *dressage* with Iberian horses. We spent hours in conversation and study with the famous *ecuyer* Jean-Philippe Giacomini, Director of Trophaeum Mundi International, discussing the spiritual nature of Iberian horses and how a transcendental process occurs between horse and rider when heart and soul are opened through the rider. José Risso Montes, a Peruvian *caballero* and international judge and trainer specializing in Peruvian horses, also concurs with this esoteric philosophy. He maintains that to ride properly and artistically, riders must get out of their intellects and only ride with their hearts and souls. We all agree on the vital importance of interior riding and training. Riding with passion, with the interior self, is the path to mysticism.

Mystical Union

To become a centaur, we advance farther on the spiritual road. We no longer experience distance. Two distinct and separate beings join and become one. There is no differentiation between human and horse: we are the dancer and the dance. This is a very difficult and challenging process. If the rider manages to achieve this oneness with the horse, in the beginning it is typically a fleeting but indelible experience. Suspending intellect is what allows a human mind to unite with the mind of a horse and to enter the realm of pure feeling. To begin the metamorphosis, riders must feel secure enough, both mentally and physically, to stop imposing their will. Trusting the horse is crucial and sparks intimacy. When trust occurs at this level, our humanmade fears disappear and the horse responds lovingly with great elation. The love and unity are art. What often demarcates such a union is that the fruits of the relationship become luminous.

Reaching this degree of intimacy happens when healthy play is freely exercised. The preparation, however, takes time, discipline and commitment. This gives us the opportunity to build a psychic structure with the necessary flexibility to eventually let go, to experience a little death. Although this accomplishment is rare and seldom achieved in our intellectual world, it is also one important goal of depth psychotherapy. It is this successive experience of symbolic death and rebirth that leads to the creative crescendo.

The principles are the same on a horse. Each participant must learn the basic skills and mechanics and achieve a modicum of competence and confidence before achieving a taste of becoming the centaur. This feeling can also be aroused without riding by participating in a vicarious way through imaginative channels, by developing a connective feeling with horses. When the horse senses you are ready for freedom, it lets you know by its expression. Until then it simply errs on the side of caution and holds back.

On a horse, letting go must have a mental and spiritual component. Everything you do must be done with pure intentions, free from malice, and in the spirit of complete love, trust and confidence. This is when telepathic communication begins. The merging begins with an inner feeling of complete peace. As we relax our human defenses, becoming less vigilant, our senses become more acute. Everything around us becomes heightened. We become more sensitive to the various aspects of the experience, such as the sound of horses' hooves hitting the ground, their muscle movement, their breathing. We begin to meditate on the inner energy of the horse. We begin to meld with the horse by waves of sensation. Nonetheless, we can still find remnants of our intellectual processes as we feel our seat in the saddle and our legs on the flanks of the animal. However, as we go deeper into the unconscious we feel our seat, hipbones and legs being absorbed into the body of the horse. Then our upper torso and arms disappear as well. Interestingly, the last to go is usually our hands because they are the human symbol of mastery, control, conquest, domination and power. Finally, we are out of our body and we are the horse. Our mind is its mind, and we are one. The entity we have created explodes with creativity.

This leaves us in a state of pure feeling. The Greek word for this is *extasis*, meaning "to get outside of oneself," to free oneself from the shackles of rationality. According to John Sanford, due to the confines of our ego, we rely predominantly on our five senses for knowledge and adhere to fact. Logic has its advantages, but if the soul never gets a respite, it feels imprisoned. He continues, "Then the soul longs to burst out of what has become a prison and merge with the Divine." This periodic freedom is ecstasy, and to find healthy avenues to exercise it invigorates and nourishes the soul. "At one time it was one of the main functions of religion to help people find true ecstasy, that is, to offer ways in which a person could leave for the time being the usual boundaries and structures in which we are for the most part confined, so we could, through ecstasy, find a transforming and enlivening relationship with the creative powers within us." [4]

No one ever really masters "the dance," but they begin to feel the music of nature. Nonetheless, experiences of this kind with horses allow us to enter their circle of light.

Exercising the Spirit with Horses

Because horses are such magical creatures, learning to dance with them is a powerful and transforming experience. It introduces nuance into our lives, ultimately enriching our spiritual core. Artistic collaboration with a horse invokes the musical experience created when melody, rhythm, harmony, timbre and form coalesce into a coherent whole. In learning the art of horsemanship, we embrace these same elements and also become whole.

Although intricate dance maneuvers on horseback involve a rider's advanced psychospiritual tools, so do less complicated exercises. You don't have to be an accomplished equestrian to learn about the hidden, or mystical, aspects of horsemanship. The only prerequisite is that you have desire and commitment to learn. The process is analogous to the alchemist's seeking to extract spiritual elements from physical matter. This quest challenges our ability to go beyond our physical senses into the realm of the intuitive. The student must not only master movement technique but, more important, animate the process, or imbue it with spirit. This task is often difficult unless we adopt a new mental paradigm.

The equine program offers people a concrete way of seeing some of these esoteric principles in action. The activities themselves help us become less intellectually constricted and move into a more soulful mind frame. They get us to occupy our bodies more fully. Master *ecuyer* Dominique Barbier maintains there is a way of calming your intellect and letting your animal mind come up so you can become one with the horse. We agree.

Artists of Life

Mastering an art form is a lifelong process that tests our ability to transcend the mundane and fully gain access to our creative core. Italian psychiatrist Silvano Arieti said of the subject of creativity and how it influences the developing human soul, "Creativity, a prerogative of man, can be seen as the humble human counterpart of God's creation. . . . But the creative process goes beyond the usual means of dealing with the environment or with oneself. It brings about what is considered—by some people, at least, and perhaps by all—a desirable enlargement of the human experience. . . . Creative work thus may have a dual role: at the same time as it enlarges the universe by adding or uncovering new dimensions, it also enriches and expands man, who will be able to experience these new dimensions inwardly." [5]

Interestingly, attaining technical expertise doesn't mean that the technician has reached a creative pinnacle. In working with people and horses, we've observed that even those highly accomplished riders who've spent years honing their horsemanship run into psychological obstacles. Although the rider typically perceives such an obstacle as a crisis, it's often actually the prelude to emergence into a new artistic level of mastery. The key is to seize these experiences and transform them into moments of truth and triumph.

Imbalances in a rider's character or behavior interfere with a horse's freedom of movement. The horse's aesthetic appearance is a fairly accurate indicator of its rider's level of personal development, which is reflected in the artistic aspects of riding performance. Working in this arena reveals where we are on the continuum, which extends from being austere and mechanically oriented to being a romantic who enjoys ascending into realms of beauty.

Beholding Beauty

To understand and connect with horses in a deep way, we have to shift our pessimistic frame of mind. Anxiety, worry, doom, anger and a host of other like feelings transfer from rider to horse. Developing a lightheartedness helps the horse cope with the rider's emotional state. Actively directing our energy in positive ways is part of this process because the horse follows it.

The key is to acquire the ability to alter our negativity. To do this we use our capacity to project, but in a healthy way. Instead of expelling negative feelings and thoughts onto the world, we project good ones. Envisioning beauty and love in our mind's eye accomplishes this end. Then we create a lighter psychological paradigm.

A story by one of our riding students describes the energy exchange between rider and horse:

> During one of my lessons I had a straightforward and amusing experience teaching me how keen horses are to our

mental flow or vibrations. For a variety of reasons, on that day I was unusually nervous. Rather than examine my uneasiness and shift gears and focus, I displaced my energy and fixated on some large flower pots that were being used as decoration in the arena. Each time I sailed around the ring, I reminded myself to stay away from those flower pots. Sure enough, the more I told myself to be careful, the more the horse moved closer and closer, until he was practically hugging the pots. The huge arena I was working in virtually shrank. Since the episode was anything but subtle, it was easy for me to see how the horse simply follows our path of energy. To remedy the situation, I had to imagine and visualize by way of thought and feeling that I was working in another space. By projecting a new image, I created a new reality. The horse perceived the shift and without any other communication, he was again using the entire expanse.

We have the power to elevate our thoughts, feelings and images, and when we teach ourselves how to behold beauty, we become increasingly sensitive to it.

The determining factor in attaining artistic levels of performance with a horse is the heart and soul of the rider. Under the direction of one rider, the horse might emerge as a vibrant star. The same horse in different hands can look like a lumbering machine. These differences can be visible and dramatic. Unless one feels truly whole and comfortable with his or her own animal nature, the horse will refuse to come alive.

The God in Us

In *An Introduction to Jung's Psychology*, Frieda Fordham tells us, "The feeling of godliness, of being a superman, which comes through inflation is an illusion. We may for a brief time possess phenomenal courage, or be infinitely wise or forgiving, but this is something 'beyond ourselves', and something that we cannot muster at will. We do not really understand the forces that move human beings in this way, and an attitude of humility in the face of them is absolutely necessary. But if the ego can relinquish some of the belief in its own omnipotence, a position can be found somewhere between that of consciousness with its hardly-won values, and unconsciousness with its vitality and power, and a new centre of personality can emerge, differing in its nature from the ego-centre."[6]

Dancing with the horse offers us the opportunity to meet our own inner God. Through our interactions with the horse, we can discover what kind of God lurks within us—whether it is wise, honest and loving, or wrathful and punishing. Each of us unconsciously behaves toward the horse in the same fashion as we do the world. The scenarios we act out with the animal dramatize and magnify our inner struggles.

Carl Jung held that human spiritual and religious strivings represent an instinctual drive that is every bit as strong as our other, more survival-related drives. Nonetheless, we rarely closely examine our concepts about God or a higher power. In the equestrian arena, each rider or handler acts as creative director. As such, each of us provides our own model for exploring the God archetype.

Handling horses stirs up issues of omnipotence for many riders and provides an opportunity to observe how easy it is to succumb to the "dark side." We can be seduced by our own sense of power into working in conflict with the horse, using force, dominance and anger as tools instead of working in concert with the animal and using disciplined kindness.

Self-Scrutiny, or Purgatory

The only way we know of to effectively rid ourselves of an out-of-control ego is, unfortunately, through suffering. Periods of crisis, during which we recognize that our ego is inclined to be seduced and become inflated, offer opportunities for substantial change, for reevaluating oneself and one's situation. These periods can be thought of as a form of purgatory. Originally the word "purgatory" referred to a time of healing because it involved purging—facing problems, making amends, seeking forgiveness and learning from life's experiences. In this sense, purgatory is a form of catharsis. Spending time in this way station ensured entry into the metaphysical realm. The transitory stay in purgatory is also influenced by the laws of karma. You feel the impact your actions have on another, as if you are that other. It is a powerful lesson on empathy, and it applies to your actions with horses as it does to your actions with all sentient beings.

Any attempts to circumvent genuine collaboration with a horse through bullying, relying on the intellect, passivity or other manipulative strategy are met with disdain. This is not to say that we don't need to exercise some degree of domination. It simply must be exercised honestly and with sensitivity. One of our students stated it in the following way: "Perhaps working with horses is a way to walk the middle way between being led and leading, between being in control and being out of control. Riding exercises the middle way, the Tao, yet establishes one's lead, exercising the internal lead mechanism."

Our work with a client named Lois illustrates this principle well. She enrolled in the equine program to make progress in personal and spiritual growth. The horse she worked with consistently tried to please her, but Lois was never satisfied. Nothing was enough, and she offered little praise or encouragement. Finally, the horse developed a habit, which he acted out only in her presence. Every time she rode, the horse would slow down and peter out or come to a complete halt. After several days of this, Lois grew impatient and resentful.

As far as we could determine, the horse's behavior was perfectly in sync with that of his rider. Lois didn't enjoy being on the other end of this exchange—a form of purgatory she herself had created—and came to realize that she didn't admire the same lack of generosity in herself. After achieving this insight, Lois decided that if she really wanted to connect with the divine, she had best develop a more giving spirit.

Avoiding Purgatory

If individuals engage in activities to control others but not to learn about themselves, it shows when they are around horses. One woman client wanted to improve her marital relationship. She and her husband were feeling estranged. She started riding because she wanted to have an activity they could participate in together. She said she loved horses and worked with them religiously. Seeing her newfound interest, her husband became interested as well. Her husband was new to horses but once exposed, showed real enthusiasm and talent. When she discovered this, rather than feeling a bond, she stopped riding. We learned she went on to a new hobby, something that her husband had no interest in. She had become involved in horses for the wrong reason. Instead of making a bond, she was trying to gain a feeling of dominance over her husband, hoping to be better than he. Her desire to be an accomplished horsewoman dwindled when she learned her husband had a natural proclivity in this area. When her fantasy burst, she moved on. He continues his riding, and they are now separated. She refused counseling on or off a horse.

Another client was learning to ride because she felt an affinity with horses and wanted to pursue it. Joan would be intensely involved with her lesson when all of a sudden, she would jump abruptly off the horse and say, "That's enough now." The horse always felt puzzled, wondering what was going on, and so did we. Joan was out of sync with the feelings of the horse but never gave her odd behavior a second thought.

Going so far, and then for some unknown reason quitting, had been a lifelong pattern. Although this behavior was strange, Joan could never see that what she was doing on a horse was a common theme in her life. Being unwilling or unable to observe herself, she continued to do things in her own idiosyncratic way. She was unable to make a bridge outside of her paradigm and see the relevance of riding to life. She was always quick to say, "These are just animals. What do they know? My problems are at work and with people." So she remained in the dark. Joan continued to wonder why she was never promoted at her job, although she had superior skills, and why her friends eventually moved on. Her style was to mold everything to her fixed design, whether it worked or not. The horses did not help her because she never listened to them.

Until recently, purgatory represented a sanctuary for learning and self-discovery rather than a place for punishment. Still, for those who believe in reincarnation, it is something one can carry into the next life.

Redemption

Once we see our inner world materialize through the medium of the horse and feel the repercussions, we can begin the process of letting go. The horse usually sets this in motion by zeroing in on and exposing our character. Our inner substance comes into sharp focus.

Those who are serious about gaining perspective on central issues in their lives and about cultivating their spiritual being will usually work very hard to meet these goals. They quickly learn that success in this endeavor starts with approaching the horse with respect, honesty and openness. This requires that they surrender any anger, bitterness, hatred, perfectionism, aimlessness or anything else that will interfere with the process of transformation. In short, they have to be present. The focus can then shift from ego gratification to the intangible, more meaningful aspects of life.

One of our clients, a talented, successful businesswoman, wanted to be a writer. Sarah's problem was that she would have brief, intermittent flashes of inspiration between long bouts of writer's block. She was afraid that her creative well was running dry. Sarah hoped that through working with us and the horses, she could unlock her creativity and get past the writer's block.

When we first began working together, Sarah was insecure and disappointed in her own abilities. Although she was unaware of it at the time, she was feeling very drained. She was operating on automatic pilot and unaware of feeling depleted.

Sarah mastered fundamental riding skills quickly. She not only loved the horses but was ambitious, conscientious and masterful at conceptualizing the mechanics and kinetics of each exercise. She advanced to a quite adequate level of expertise rather quickly.

On the surface, Sarah appeared composed. Nonetheless, as her proficiency grew, so did the creative demands of progressively more difficult tasks. This began to show. Sarah was now encountering another dimension of riding, one that calls for extrasensory forms of communication like telepathy and creative visualization, which produce a hypnotic union between horse and rider.

She was also being asked to relate in a more selfless way to the animal and encourage him to express more of his exuberance. Having difficulty with this ability to be more playful, she resorted to coercion. Rather than learning to develop her metaphysical abilities, she tried to take the path of least resistance and physically maneuver the horse through these exercises.

In no time at all, the stage turned into a battlefield rather than a forum for the dance. She became childishly demanding, stubborn and compulsive. Conquering her inadequacies became paramount, to the exclusion of everything else. She was driven to get it right, and her practice sessions deteriorated into mechanical drills, the endless practice into a "nice" way of punishing the horse for making her look bad. Interestingly enough, the horse never fought back aggressively but countered her passively with the same iron will.

One day it dawned on her that they were at a serious impasse. Never giving the horse a chance to acquiesce but squeezing out of him what she desired was a mistake. She had forgotten that he was an equal partner and would give willingly, if she would politely ask. This simple notion was a revelation to her. Her relationship with the horse changed dramatically as soon as she acknowledged his presence and asked for this participation. When he graciously responded, she reported a feeling of being enveloped by an all-giving benevolent force. She also recognized that she had bypassed this love by habitually using her intellect during times of stress. She alone had turned the universe into a desolate and withholding place. Following her breakthrough on this horse, her attitude changed. Now the passage from the New Testament in the Book of Matthew made sense to her: "Ask, it will be given to you; seek, and you will find; knock, and it will be opened to you." When she finally asked, this abundance became readily available because she had worked so diligently.

Sarah came to understand that being rigid killed her creative flow, closing her mind off to the movement of the cosmos. When she finally began to loosen her stranglehold, some of the finest moments between her and the horse occurred, in reverie.

CONCLUSION

The horse is man's most noble conquest.

—Buffon, *Reflections on Equestrian Art*

Nature is an all-encompassing force, embodying both male and female, good and evil, dark and light, beginning and end. It is the totality of experience—not only a well of creativity but an abyss of destruction. It is through our experience with Nature that we are confronted with the two basic elements of existence—creation and death—whose volatility we so often deny.

Throughout history, the wild variation of experience in Nature has earned her the title "Goddess of Wisdom." Across cultures, she is called by different names. Gnostic Christians know her as Sophia. The Hindus call her Kali.

In *The Dancing Wu Li Masters*, Gary Zukav writes, "In Hindu mythology, Kali, the Divine Mother, is the symbol for the infinite diversity of experience. Kali represents the entire physical plane. She is drama, tragedy, humor, and sorrow of life. She is the brother, father, sister, mother, lover and friend.

She is the fiend, monster, beast and brute. She is the sun and the ocean. She is the grass and the dew. She is our sense of accomplishment and our sense of doing worthwhile. Our thrill of discovery is a pendant on her bracelet. Our gratification is a spot of color on her cheek. Our sense of importance is the bell on her toe. This full and seductive, terrible and wonderful earth mother always has something to offer. Hindus know the impossibility of seducing or conquering her and the futility of loving or hating her; so they do the only thing they can do. They simply honor her." [1]

Horses serve as our link to nature. We feel it's ironic that, prior to the journey we have described here, we considered ourselves "nature lovers." Actually, we had walked through her but were never truly with her. Over many years, we learned that there is a vast distinction. When our journey began, we were outsiders looking in. As time passed, we walked with Mother Nature. As we emerge from our pilgrimage, we know that we are Nature. All signposts now point in one direction—home.

The path we propose is no easy one, but to continue growing as human beings and occupants of this planet, we cannot limit our development to the material plane of existence. We must find ways to soar to unseen dimensions. That flight begins with our imaginations. We must reach beyond the possible to the impossible, and touch the untouchable.

Why do so many of us limit our vision to narrow prisons? Why do we dismantle our dreams? We have allowed ourselves to become technicians in life, rather than life itself. We must wake up and realize that we are not just acted upon by the force, but are ourselves part of the force, acting upon ourselves and others.

To deny that we are Nature is to produce great suffering. We can all see the result in this separatist world we have constructed. In a cocoon of our own weaving, we ignore the laws of nature. What are the consequences? Increasing violence, crime, gangs, mental illness, divorce, polarized hostility between the sexes and every other us/them division, not to mention the damage we are inflicting on our environment. We also lose the meaning of our existence and begin just to exist rather than living fully and joyfully.

Manifestations of personal disintegration, such as increasing deviance and an increase in the number of psychotic and psychopathic people, tell us that the problems we now face as a society are not "out there" somewhere. They are in our hearts. If we would see ourselves as a fraction of the whole and as part of one another, perhaps we would begin with ourselves and stop trying to fix everyone else. To acknowledge that each of us is part perpetrator, part angel, is a first step in finding dynamic cures to what ails us. We are responsible for the world we live in.

The next time a problem emerges in your life, instead of looking for someone else to blame, ask yourself, "Why did I dance?" Despite the elaborate rationales we concoct, the fact remains that accepting the invitation to dance sets the stage for the course of events to follow. To change the course, we must acknowledge our participation and the cold, hard truth that each of us builds our own life, dance by dance, step by step, through our own choices. This position is unpopular today because it means we must all stop complaining and ask instead, "What can I learn from this?"

Interaction with our horses forced us to look beyond pat solutions from outside ourselves and to direct our attention inward for our answers. Nature, represented so eloquently by horses, has much to teach us. Listening to her can start us on the path to viewing ourselves and the world as a whole, rather than as separate, distinct parts. By letting nature reflect back to us the essence of our own creation, we find our way to our lost inner selves and the sense of connection and excitement missing in our lives. We are still at work and learning.

NOTES

FOREWORD

1. *British Columbia Times-Colonist*, 22 August 1996.

2. Dennis Bardens, *Psychic Animals* (New York: Barnes & Noble, 1996), 179.

3. Bardens, 13-14.

4. Bardens, 14.

5. *Daily Telegraph*, 27 August 1996.

6. *Daily Telegraph*, 30 August 1996.

7. Samuel Butler, quoted in T. Friend, "Cagemates: Why Animals and Humans Can't Escape Each Other," *Utne Reader*, Jan.-Feb. 1996: 62-64.

8. Amit Goswami, "The Idealistic Interpretation of Quantum Mechanics," *Physics Essays* 2.4 (1989): 385-99.

9. From a discussion of Rupert Sheldrake's thought, in Larry Dossey, *Recovering the Soul: A Scientific and Spiritual Search* (New York: Bantam Books, 1989), 206.

10. See Dossey, *Recovering the Soul*, for a thorough introduction to the concepts of nonlocality and human consciousness.

11. George Jaidar, *The Soul: An Owner's Manual* (St. Paul, Minn.: Paragon House, 1995), 34.

CHAPTER 2: OUR CONNECTION WITH ANIMALS

1. John A. Sanford, *Mystical Christianity: A Psychological Commentary on the Gospel of John* (New York: Crossroad, 1994), 244-45.

2. Constantin Stanislavski, trans. by Elizabeth Reynolds Hapgood, *Building a Character* (New York: Hapgood Methuen Theater Arts Books, 1949), 238.

3. Robert Eisler, *Man into Wolf: An Anthropological Interpretation of Sadism, Masochism and Lycanthropy* (London: Spring Books, n.d.), 34.

CHAPTER 3: THE HEALING HORSE

1. Jean-Philippe Giacomini, *The Classic Dressage Master Class* (Houston, Tex. and San Ysidro, Calif.: Trophaeum Mundi International, 1995), 37.

CHAPTER 4: RIDING HORSES TO HEALTH

1. Sidney Rosen, M.D., *My Voice Will Go with You: The Teaching Tales of Milton H. Erickson, M.D.* (New York: W.W. Norton, 1982), 27.

2. Karl König, *Elephants, Bears, Horses, Cats and Dogs* (Edinburgh: Floris Books, 1992), 107, 110-11.

CHAPTER 6: INSTINCTS AND INTUITION

1. Rupert Sheldrake, Ph.D., *The Presence of the Past: Morphic Resonance and the Habits of Nature* (Rochester, Vt.: Park Street Press, 1988), 221.

CHAPTER 7: TAMING THE INSTINCTS

1. Carl G. Jung and M.-L. von Franz, Joseph L. Henderson, Jolande Jacobi, and Aniela Jaffé. *Man and His Symbols* (New York: Doubleday & Company, Inc., 1964), 31.

CHAPTER 8: DISCIPLINED PLAY

1. Hilary Sandall, "The Psychiatrist and Chronic Mental Illness," *Psychiatric Annals* 10 (Sept. 1980): 9.

2. Simon A. Grolnick, M.D., and Leonard Barkin, M.D., in collaboration with Werner Muensterberger, Ph.D., eds., *Between Reality and Fantasy: Transitional Objects and Phenomena* (New York: Jason Aronson, Inc., 1978), 374.

3. Rosen, 27.

4. Jung et al., 20, 21, 23.

CHAPTER 10: SPIRITUALITY

1. Peter Tompkins and Christopher Bird, *The Secret Life of Plants* (New York: Avon Books, 1973), 216.

2. Jiddu Krishnamurti, *You Are the World: An Authentic Report of Talks and Discussions in American Universities* (New York: Harper and Row, 1973, reissued 1989), 62.

3. Rudolf Steiner, *Psychoanalysis and Spiritual Psychology* (New York: Anthroposophic Press, Inc., 1990), 111.

4. Sanford, 284-85.

5. Silvano Arieti, M.D., *Creativity: The Magic Synthesis* (New York: Basic Books/Harper Colophon Books, 1976), 5.

6. Frieda Fordham, *An Introduction to Jung's Psychology* (Harmondsworth, Middlesex, England: Penguin Books, 1966), 61-62.

CONCLUSION

1. Gary Zukav, *The Dancing Wu Li Masters: An Overview of the New Physics* (New York: Bantam Books, 1979), 311-12.

BIBLIOGRAPHY

Arieti, Silvano. *Creativity: The Magic Synthesis*. New York: Basic Books, Inc./Harper Colophon Books, 1976.

Barbier, Dominique. *Dressage for the New Age*. New York: Prentice-Hall, 1990.

Blake, Henry. *Talking with Horses: A Study of Communication Between Man and Horse*. North Pomfret, Vt.: Trafalgar Square Publishing, 1990.

Campbell, Joseph. *The Masks of God: Creative Mythology*. New York: Arkana, 1968.

Dossey, Larry, M.D. *Recovering the Soul: A Scientific and Spiritual Search*. New York: Bantam Books, 1989.

Eisler, Robert. *Man into Wolf: An Anthropological Interpretation of Sadism, Masochism and Lycanthropy*. London: Spring Books, n.d.

Erikson, Erik H. *Identity, Youth and Crisis*. New York: W.W. Norton and Co., Inc., 1968.

Fordham, Frieda. *An Introduction to Jung's Psychology*. Harmondsworth, Middlesex, England: Penguin Books, 1966.

Fox, Matthew. *The Coming of the Cosmic Christ: The Healing of Mother Earth and the Birth of Global Renaissance*. San Francisco: Harper, 1988.

Giacomini, J. P. *The Classic Dressage Master Class*. Houston, Tex., and San Ysidro, Calif.: Trophaeum Mundi International, 1995.

Grolnick, Simon, M.D. *The Work and Play of Winnicott*. Northvale, N.J.: Jason Aronson, Inc., 1990.

Grolnick, Simon A., M.D., and Leonard Barkin, MD., in collaboration with Werner Muensterberger, Ph.D., eds. *Between Reality and Fantasy: Transitional Objects and Phenomena*. New York: Jason Aronson, Inc., 1978.

Holy Bible: The New King James Version. Nashville: Thomas Nelson Publishers, 1992.

Jung, Carl G., and M.-L. von Franz, Joseph L. Henderson, Jolande Jacobi, Aniela Jaffé. *Man and His Symbols*. New York: Doubleday & Company, Inc., 1964.

König, Karl. *Elephants, Bears, Horses, Cats and Dogs*. Edinburgh: Floris Books, 1992.

Kowalski, Gary. "Do Animals Have Souls?" *Creation Spirituality*, Jan.-Feb. 1993: 21-23.

Krishnamurti, Jiddu. *You Are the World: An Authentic Report of Talks and Discussions in American Universities*. New York: Harper and Row, 1972, reissued 1989.

———. *On Mind and Thought*. San Francisco: Harper Collins, 1993.

Moreno, Jacob Levy, M.D. *Psychodrama: Volume I*. Beacon, N.Y.: Beacon House, Inc., 1964.

Morse, Melvin, M.D. *Closer to the Light*. New York: Ivy Books-Ballantine Books, 1990.

Rees, Lucy. *The Horse's Mind*. New York: Arco Publishing, Inc., 1984.

Reich, Wilhelm. *Character Analysis*. New York: Simon & Schuster, 1972.

Rosen, Sidney, ed. *My Voice Will Go with You: The Teaching Tales of Milton H. Erickson, M.D.* New York: W.W. Norton, 1982.

Sandall, Hilary. "The Psychiatrist and Chronic Mental Illness." *Psychiatric Annals*, Sept. 1980, 10:9.

Sanford, John A. *Mystical Christianity: A Psychological Commentary on the Gospel of John*. New York: Crossroad, 1994.

Sheldrake, Rupert, Ph.D. *The Presence of the Past: Morphic Resonance and the Habits of Nature*. Rochester, Vt.: Park Street Press, 1988, reissued 1995.

Stanislavski, Constantin, translated by Elizabeth Reynolds Hapgood. *Building a Character*. New York: Hapgood Methuen Theater Arts Books, 1949.

Steiner, Rudolph. *Psychoanalysis and Spiritual Psychology*. New York: Anthroposophic Press, Inc., 1990.

Taylor, Eugene, ed. *William James on Exceptional Mental States, from the 1896 Lowell Lectures*. New York: Scribner and Sons, 1983.

Thass-Thienemann, Theodore. *The Interpretation of Language: Volume I, Understanding the Symbolic Meaning of Language*. New York: Jason Aronson, Inc., 1973.

———. *The Interpretation of Language: Volume II, Understanding the Unconscious Meaning of Language*. New York: Jason Aronson, Inc., 1973.

Tompkins, Peter, and Christopher Bird. *The Secret Life of Plants*. New York: Avon Books, 1973.

Yogananda, Paramahansa. *Autobiography of a Yogi*. Los Angeles: Self-Realization Fellowship, 1993.

Zukav, Gary. *The Dancing Wu Li Masters: An Overview of the New Physics*. New York: Bantam Books, 1979.

Zweig, Connie, and Jeremiah Abrams, eds. *Meeting the Shadow, The Hidden Power of the Dark Side of Human Nature*. New York: Putnam, 1991.

INDEX

ABOUT THE AUTHORS

Adele von Rüst McCormick, Ph.D., and Marlena Deborah McCormick, Ph.D., have been psychotherapists for more than 30 years, designing and running a series of unique and innovative programs for criminals, people with mental illness, and individuals with drug and alcohol problems. Currently, they are codirectors of the Institute for Conscious/Awareness and cofounders of the Three Eagles Equine Experience in San Antonio, Texas, which offers courses using horsemanship to open spirituality and intuition for individuals, families or groups.

For more information contact:

The Institute for Conscious/Awareness
16608 San Pedro
Suite 107
San Antonio, TX 78232
Phone: 830-438-2816
E-mail: thomasm@gvtc.com

New from the *Chicken Soup for the Soul*® Serie

Chicken Soup for the Teenage Soul

Teens welcome *Chicken Soup for the Teenage Soul* like a
good friend: one who understands their feelings, is there
for them when needed and cheers them up when things are
looking down. A wonderful gift for your teenage son,
daughter, grandchild, student, friend... #4630—$12.95

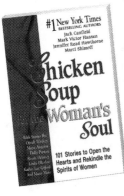

Chicken Soup for the Woman's Soul

The #1 *New York Times* bestseller guaranteed to inspire
women with wisdom and insights that are uniquely femi-
nine and always from the heart. #4150—$12.95

Chicken Soup for the Christian Soul

Chicken Soup for the Christian Soul is an inspiring
reminder that we are never alone or without hope, no
matter how challenging or difficult our life may seem.
In God we find hope, healing, comfort and love.
#5017—$12.95

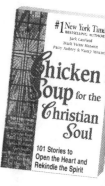

Chicken Soup for the Soul® Series

Each one of these inspiring *New York Times* bestsellers brings you
exceptional stories, tales and verses guaranteed to lift your spirits
soothe your soul and warm your heart! A perfect gift for anyone
you love, including yourself!

A 4th Course of Chicken Soup for the Soul, #4592—$12.95
A 3rd Serving of Chicken Soup for the Soul, #3790—$12.95
A 2nd Helping of Chicken Soup for the Soul, #3316—$12.95
Chicken Soup for the Soul, #262X—$12.95

Selected books are also available in hardcover, large print,
audiocassette and compact disc.

Available in bookstores everywhere or call **1-800-441-5569** for Visa or
MasterCard orders. Prices do not include shipping and handling.
Your response code is **HORSE**.